**Books are to be returned on or before
the last date below**

Coins

COINS

Andrew Burnett

Published for the Trustees of the British Museum
by British Museum Press

I would like to thank Roger Bland, Barrie Cook, Joe Cribb, Kenneth W. Harl, Nina Shandloff, Celia Clear and Ruth Baldwin for their help. The photographs were taken by Chaz Howson and the drawings were made by Noelle Derrett.

Designed by Andrew Shoolbred

Set in Linotron Palatino and printed in
Great Britain by The Bath Press, Avon

British Library Cataloguing in Publication Data
Burnett, Andrew
    Coins.
    1. Coins, history
    I. Title
    737.409

ISBN 0–7141–2059–6

Cover illustration: Some of the coins (before and after conservation) from a hoard of Roman silver coins and finger rings. The hoard was discovered at Silchester, Hampshire, and dates to *c.* AD 410.

Contents

Preface

Coins are one of the most important sources of information from which archaeologists and historians can try to interpret the past. This is not simply because, unlike most other artefacts, they are often stamped with words, images and even dates, but also because of their quantity and durability.

Huge numbers of coins survive from past societies dating back over two thousand years. For instance, the British Museum has a collection of well over half a million, and something like 30,000 are unearthed every year in Britain alone. Being made of metal, often precious metal, coins have tended to survive much better than less durable objects. Because they are a form of money they have often been concealed for safe-keeping in hoards, and such careful burial has contributed to the excellent state of preservation today of so many objects made hundreds of years ago.

Unlike most objects studied by archaeologists, coins were officially produced by the state rather than privately made by individuals. This means the type of information they can give is often different from that of other artefacts. Their designs and inscriptions, for instance, are an unrivalled source of systematic detail relating to political history, religion and culture. Their role as the principal form of money for over two millennia means they can tell us about economies for which we have little or no written evidence, and the fact that they were mass-produced and have survived in such large numbers offers the opportunity to approach the economic history of some societies in a quantitative way.

Underpinning both the interpretation of their designs and the economic evidence they can provide is the datability of coins. Their high survival rate and their official inscriptions have combined to make them the most easily and most accurately datable of all archaeological artefacts.

For all these reasons, coins are an essential tool for the archaeologist and the historian in extending our knowledge of the past. Since the historical study of coins began, in the Italian Renaissance, many different methods have been developed, particularly within the last century, and the most important of these are considered in the following pages. The text is illustrated with examples drawn mainly from the Roman world, although different examples from other periods and cultures could easily have been used instead. It is not the purpose of this book to provide a history of coinage, however brief, but rather to focus on the methods by which coins are studied, for only when these methods are properly understood and applied can we realise the full potential of coins as an aid to interpreting the past.

— 1 —

What are Coins?

A coin is a piece of money made out of metal, usually gold, silver or some copper alloy. We all take the use of coins for granted, but they have not been made or used by all metalworking societies. Coinage was invented only comparatively late in human history. The main, Western tradition began only in about 600 BC in Asia Minor and spread to cover most of Europe, the Mediterranean world and Asia as far as India; a separate Eastern tradition came into being in China in about the sixth century BC. This latter tradition remained geographically confined to the Far East and continued to flourish until it was gradually replaced, from the eighteenth century AD, by Western-style coinage.

None of the great early Near Eastern societies, such as those of the Sumerians, the Hittites or Pharaonic Egypt, had coins. And, even after the invention of coinage, many areas or cities did not use it. For example, despite the prevalence of coinage in ancient Greece, one of the great powers, Sparta, did not adopt it until well after the heyday of Spartan power. Great trading nations such as the Phoenicians and the Etruscans produced almost no coins. The Persian empire made and used coins only in the part of its territory which adjoined the coin-using lands of Greece. The Romans started to make coins only in about 300 BC. Coinage was almost unknown in Britain for over two hundred years, between the Roman abandonment of the province in about AD 400 and the beginnings of medieval coinage in the seventh century. The use of coinage was also abandoned in Russia from the twelfth to the early fourteenth century, and in Japan from the tenth to the fourteenth century.

All these societies were more or less developed economically, but did not use coinage. Other forms of money were used, such as animals or units of metal by weight. But coinage has, until recently, been the most common and frequently used form of money because it is so convenient, portable and durable. Coinage can also perform all the common functions of money, of which there are several in a typical market-based economy. Money may, for example, be used as a measure of value enabling comparisons of value to be made between different objects such as houses or cattle. It may function as a store of wealth, so that an individual or society can put away the wealth it may generate as the surplus between production and consumption. Third, money can function as a medium of exchange, as a physical object which facilitates the exchange of goods (or the fulfilment of social obligations) between different parties.

But, if units of metal have been used as monetary values and in monetary transactions, what is the difference between a coin and a lump of metal? It is not that the coin is of a fixed weight, since lumps of bullion can and often are produced to a specific weight standard. It is not that it has a design stamped on it, since once again it is not difficult to find other examples of metalwork decorated in a similar way. It is not the fact that a coin is often worth more than the value of the bullion it contains. This has indeed usually been the case: for instance, in ancient Greece where the value of a silver coin was generally 5 per cent greater than an equivalent weight of silver (to cover costs of minting and profit to the mint). But not all coins have been overvalued in this way; for example, late Roman gold coins of the fourth century AD and British sovereigns of the nineteenth century were literally worth their weight in gold.

The differentiating characteristic of a coin as opposed to a piece of bullion is that it is issued with a recognised value by a competent authority. This authority is normally the sovereign body in the state, such as a king or popular assembly, although in practice this authority might be delegated to or assumed by another body or individual.

There are various reasons why authorities might choose to issue coins, although the common factor is that there would be some benefit, however indirect, to the state. In some societies coinage was minted solely in accordance with the government's instructions, in order to meet the state's requirements for public expenditure on war, army and civil service pay, food, or public buildings. At other times it has been possible for an individual to bring foreign coins or bullion to the mint and receive it back as coinage (minus a fee). This was the case sometimes in classical antiquity – for example, in Egypt in the third century BC or the Roman empire during the late fourth century AD and generally in most late medieval societies, when mints in different countries might even compete by offering better terms. In such cases there might be different sorts of motivation, such as the prestige which accrued from the production of a large coinage in the state's name or the profit which came to the state from the minting fee. On occasion arrangements would be made between governments, such as in the period 1632–47 when England and Spain agreed that large amounts of Spanish silver were to be coined at the mint of London, accounting for a high proportion of its output. In an extreme case an authority might decide for economic, political or cultural reasons that it did not wish to make coinage, which may explain the periods mentioned above when various states abandoned coinage.

The involvement of the competent authority is thus essential to the existence and nature of any coinage system. And to enable coinage to function smoothly it must be properly controlled by that authority. The state's involvement offers crucial protection, since failure to accept a coin or tampering with it in some way, like making a forgery, then is regarded as a crime against the state, and serious penalties including execution have frequently been normal for such activities. Equally important is public confidence or acceptance of coinage; as coinage is a convention, in the sense that its value is conventionally fixed by the authority of the state with the agreement of the public, it can only function if the value of the coinage, as fixed by the state, is accepted by those who use it; otherwise, market forces will tend to discount overvalued coins towards their individual bullion values.

The fact that coins are monetary objects issued by various authorities is what makes them such a valuable source of information for the historian. Obviously their monetary role can tell us much about monetary and perhaps also economic activity in any society, and this aspect will be discussed in Chapter 4. The essential involvement of an issuing authority gives the choice of the designs placed on coins a relevance to our understanding of the political aspirations or concerns of that authority, and this, together with the great wealth of illustration provided by such designs, will be discussed in Chapter 3. But, as with any archaeological object, such interpretations can be made only when we have a secure idea of when and where a coin was made, and the methods of dating coins and attributing them to mints is therefore discussed first in Chapter 2, where it will also be seen that the same techniques for dating and attributing coins can sometimes be turned round, using coins to date other objects or to identify places. In this short book it is not, of course, intended to provide a complete treatment of these themes, and readers more experienced in the subject will be aware that little space has been given, for example, to the potential of documentary sources or modern methods of study using computers and advanced statistical methods. Instead, the intention here is to concentrate on the coins themselves, showing their potential value as evidence for the past and, broadly speaking, how this evidence can be interpreted.

— 2 —

Dating and Attributing Coins

The first task with a coin, as with any other artefact, is to try to establish its date and attribute it to a place of manufacture and authority, since we must know where and when it was made before it can give us any information about the past. In this respect coins, generally speaking, give more help than other objects because they quite often declare either where or when they were made. A glance at the inscription and design of a modern coin, for instance, will nearly always tell us which state issued it and the year in which it was

1 This iron die (*left* and *below*) was made for striking gold ten-shilling coins of Charles I in 1629–30. Most medieval English dies are similar, but the few ancient dies which have survived differ somewhat in shape (more conical, no square projection) and in metal (bronze rather than iron).

2 In the ancient and medieval worlds coins were made by hand. This woodcut (*opposite*) gives an idea of the stages involved in the preparation of the blank flans and striking them with hand-held dies.

manufactured. The same is true of most Islamic coins, both of the modern and the medieval period, for Islamic rulers and states nearly always included the name of the mint and the date of manufacture as part of the design.

In other pre-modern cultures, however, it has not been usual to give all this information. The designs or inscriptions which appear on the coins made in archaic and classical Greece, for example, nearly always enable us to attribute them to one or other of the Greek city-states which made them, but none carries a date. The same is true of the coinage of medieval Europe: we can tell that a coin is, say, Spanish or English from the inscription, which usually refers to the kingdom in question, but the date may well be far from apparent. This is true even when the coin gives the name of a king. Quite apart from the habit of medieval monarchs of using a restricted number of names (e.g., Edward in England or Alfonso in Spain), it was not unusual for 'posthumous' coinages to be made in the name of a previous king. For instance, all the coins made by Richard the Lionheart and his brother John carried the name of their long-dead father, Henry II. The reason was that public confidence in the quality of the coinage depended on the retention of an 'immobilised', i.e. unchanging, design (see also p. 14 and fig. 9).

Political as well as economic reasons might contribute to the use of a standardised design. The Roman emperors of the later third century AD made very similar coins at a number of mints, and it is difficult to be sure about their correct attribution. In the same way, as the enormous empire of Alexander the Great grew in the wake of conquests made during his short reign (336–323 BC), many mints were set up, all using the same designs. These coins give no immediate clues as to their place of minting or indeed their date, for similar coinage in the name of Alexander continued to be made on a large scale for about a hundred years after his death.

For reasons such as these the numismatist is often primarily occupied with establishing the mint and date of a particular coin or group of coins. Sometimes information can be derived from written sources, such as works of history or documents, and these become more and more important from the early medieval period onwards. Documentary sources can be effective on their own or in combination with the coins themselves, but often there are no such sources. For this reason and for reasons of space, the discussion here will be confined to the way in which the coins themselves can be used to reveal information about their date or mint.

Although dating and attributing coins to mints require different methods, the preliminary step is the same in both cases. This consists of analysing the coins into groups or categories of similar coins, since it is always easier to situate a large group in place and time and then bring greater precision to an individual object forming part of that group.

Grouping coins

Typological studies

Coins can be grouped together from an examination of their designs, and different levels of precision are possible. For instance, we might sort a group of Roman coins into groups by different emperors and then subdivide these groups by some further criterion, such as the type of portrait which occurs or the inscription found with it. This commonsense method is useful for dealing with a large number of coins which are superficially similar, such as those of a long-lived Roman emperor and, particularly, 'immobilised' medieval coins. For example, the silver pennies made with identical designs under King Edward I and II can be subdivided by the form of the king's name or the shape of the crown he wears (fig. 3). The level of detail can be refined until this sort of analysis merges into one of the other main ways of grouping coins (see below).

3 The long series of 'sterling' silver pennies made in the reigns of Edward I and II (between 1279 and 1327) can be subdivided into several consecutive varieties or types. The earlier ones (*left*) abbreviate the king's name to EDW and show him wearing a crown with a triple tip; the later ones (*right*) have EDWA and a double tip.

The study of style

At the next level the detail of a design can be analysed from the point of view of style; indeed, until the twentieth century this was, with typological analysis, the principal method used in the study of coinage. Sometimes stylistic characteristics of a particular artist can be recognised, and this may allow grouping coins together. Style, however, is often misused if the approach is ill-founded or unsystematic, and such failures have tended to give it a rather poor reputation. This is a pity, since it is an important and powerful method of study as in any field of the history of art. It is therefore always desirable to spell out in detail what is meant by 'similar style'. But, even when properly used, style can be misleading. A large mint such as operated under the Roman empire might well use more than one engraver, and consequently one may find more than one style of work in use contemporaneously and at the same place. This can be seen, for example, at the Roman mint of Trier in the fourth century AD. In the same way we can now tell that there were two engravers working at the mint of Rome under the Roman Emperor Vespasian. This example is indeed a cautionary tale, as the work of the two engravers was traditionally attributed to two different mints (Rome and Tarraco, in Spain), but the discovery of numerous die links (see below) between each group has shown that they all come from the same mint.

4 Three coins of the Roman Emperor Philip (AD 244–9). The two larger coins circulated only in Syria. But the style and treatment of their portraits is very different (note the shape of the head and the alignment of the cloak). That of the second piece is very similar to the smaller coin, a denarius struck at Rome, and indicates that it too was minted at Rome and then transported to Syria. The first piece, however, was made at the local Syrian mint, at Antioch.

The study of punches

Coins were made by the process of striking a blank disc or flan of metal between two dies (see figs 1 and 2). These dies were usually made of bronze or steel, and bore the design in intaglio. In the ancient world these dies were engraved by hand, but from the early medieval period punches began to be hammered into the die to make up the designs. These punches might consist of elements of the design (such as part of the king's crown) or of letters in the inscription,

15

and a careful examination of the coins can reveal that they were struck from dies made from the same punches (fig. 5). With this method it is possible to establish an objective physical link between different coins, and it is particularly important in the study of late medieval and modern coinages.

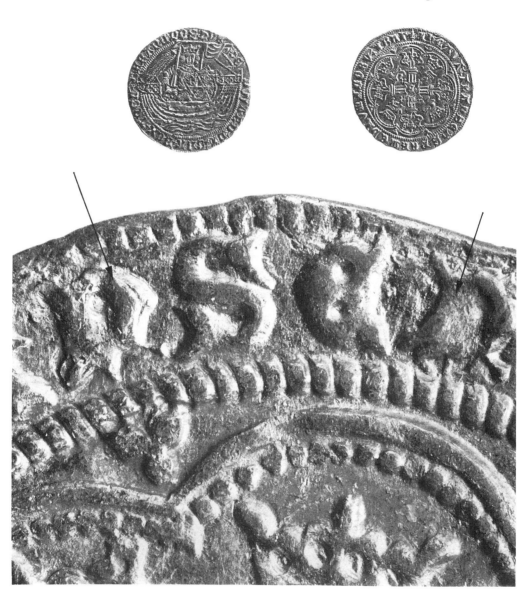

5 The same broken punch for the letter N has been used in the word TRANSENS on the die for a gold noble of Edward IV (1461–83) (*opposite*) and in the word LONDON on the die of a half-groat of the same king (*opposite below*, and *above*). This indicates that the two denominations were minted in the same part of his reign.

Die studies

The most detailed type of sorting consists of carrying out a die study. By examining the details visible on surviving coins it is possible to identify coins struck from the same die or dies, for they will show no divergence whatsoever in the details of the designs (fig. **6**). The die study has become one of the most important tools used by the numismatist because it provides a physical link

6 Two coins of Smyrna, second century BC. The coins have the head of the city-goddess and, on the reverse, a wreath enclosing the name of the city and different monograms. A close comparison of all the details of the heads reveals no differences, and shows that they were struck from the same die. Thus we can conclude that the coins and the two monograms are more or less contemporary.

between two separate objects and thereby provides evidence that they were made at the same place and time. Die studies become even more useful when, as often happens, two coins have been struck from the same die on one side but a different one on the other side. Other coins made from the same different die can often be found, thus establishing a chain of die links between objects which might otherwise display no close similarities.

This method has been used only in the twentieth century. Previously it was thought that all coins were struck from separate dies, but the increasing sophistication of photography in the late nineteenth century enabled scholars to appreciate that die links could be found, and the first full die study of the coins of a Greek city was published in 1906. The die study is nowadays the basic approach to the products of any Greek city, and indeed the coins of most periods. By performing a study of the dies and establishing a chain or chains or die links, one can arrange a whole coinage into an objective sequence. If a date can be assigned to one or more points of this relative sequence, it is normally possible to make reasonably accurate inferences about the dates of the intermediary points.

The same method of the die study is also useful in establishing mints, as die links between coins indicate that they were made at the same mint. Indeed, one of the first die links ever published drew attention to the surprising use of the same die on two coins which had been thought to be of different mints. This approach is very useful, for instance, with the coinage of Alexander mentioned on p. 14. Other examples are the Roman coinage under Vespasian (see p. 15), and particularly the many coins purporting to be English pennies of the tenth and eleventh centuries. Die links have shown that a group of pennies in the name of the English King Aethelred II and mint names of Chester, Chichester, Lincoln, London and York were in fact struck at one place, which is not located in England but perhaps in Scandinavia.

Of course, it would be much too simple if die links always proved that two objects were made at the same place and time. Indeed, we know for certain that this was sometimes not the case. A die could survive over a long period of time. For example, the dies used to make Roman bronze medallions of the second century AD might last for ten years, and at the city of Dalisandos in Asia Minor a die survived for more than eighty years. In a similar way dies were sometimes moved from one mint to another. Perhaps the clearest case is provided by the gold coinage of the Roman empire in the fifth century AD. At this period the production of gold coinage was closely associated with the presence of the imperial court, and as it moved around the empire so did some of the dies for making gold coins. Consequently, for instance, coins of the Empress Placidia were struck at Aquileia and at Rome from the same dies. But cases of die links between different places or over a long period of time are unusual. Roman medallions were made in small quantities and so the die would be likely to survive, while at Dalisandos no coinage was made in the intervening years. The unusual nature of these counter-examples indicates that they are indeed the exceptions which prove the rule, and it is normally reasonable to assume that coins made from the same die were produced at the same time and place. Indeed, where die links are found between coins of different cities, such as in southern Italy in the fourth century BC or Asia Minor in the second and third centuries AD, these links constitute good evidence for the centralised production at one mint of the coinage of several cities.

18

While these are the most important tools for the grouping together of coins, there are other subsidiary methods which can sometimes help to define groups of coins. The three principal methods, all related to the way coins were made, are based on their die axis, weight and alloy.

The first is die axis. The two dies used to strike coins were sometimes aligned in a fixed position (which might change) and sometimes were not. The relationship between the orientation of alignment of the two sides is normally expressed in hours of the clock. Thus modern British coinage has a die axis of twelve o'clock: when the coin is held above and below the Queen's head and then rotated, the design on the back appears upright or aligned at twelve o'clock. In the case of ancient or medieval coinage the existence in different groups of coins of different or similar patterns of die axis may support or reduce the likelihood of some coins belonging in the same group. Carthaginian coinage provides a good example, since the axis of coins made at Carthage was normally fixed at twelve, whereas that of coins made in the Sicilian or Sardinian provinces was variable.

Weight is another factor that can aid grouping. Coins, especially those of precious metal, were made at a particular standard of so many coins to a unit of weight (be this a Roman scripulum or an English grain). These standards can be established by weighing a sufficient number of coins on a modern balance (although there are problems in establishing ancient standards from the weight of surviving specimens). Sometimes the standard was changed, and if, for instance, we have two different standards in use in consecutive periods, we can tell from its weight to which group any new coin will belong. An example is the coinage of the Greek colonies in southern Italy, most of which reduced the weight of their silver coins by one-sixth in the early third century BC, thereby aiding in the classification of their coinages.

A similar approach can be based on an examination of the metal alloy of a coin, which can be determined by scientific analysis (see also fig. 11). Traditional chemical analysis and the measurement of specific gravity are not much used nowadays, as the former is destructive of the object and the latter is useful only when dealing with an alloy of two metals of greatly differing specific gravities; in effect this restricts its utility to alloys made of gold and one other metal. Instead various other non-destructive methods are in use today. In all these there is, generally speaking, a trade-off between the speed of analysis and the amount of information recovered. Thus, if making a rapid survey of the major elements in a group of coins, one might use X-ray fluorescence spectroscopy or a scanning electron microscope. The accurate detection range of these methods is no more than 0.05 per cent, so they are not suitable for the determination of the trace elements of a coin's alloy. To determine these it is necessary to use a slower method such as atomic absorption spectroscopy or neutron activation. In all these methods, care has to be taken with the preparation of the sample, since ancient alloys were sometimes not well mixed. A more general problem results from the distortion of the nature of the alloy on the edge of the coin through the natural processes of corrosion and surface-enrichment. As a consequence it is essential to abrade the surface of a coin (on its edge), or alternatively to drill a sample from its centre (typically using a 1- or 0.5-mm drill from the edge of the coin).

Whatever method is used, however, information about the alloy can help with its classification in cases where significant differences in alloy can be demonstrated. For example, the Roman Emperor Domitian improved the fineness of the silver denarius from 91 per cent to 98 per cent between AD 82 and 85. The discovery that otherwise enigmatic denarii struck in the name of a deified empress called Domitilla contain the higher level of silver has shown that her coins were struck in this period and not in the reign of the previous emperor, Titus. The determination of trace elements can sometimes help with mint problems. For instance, some coins of the Roman Emperor Severus Alexander found in Egypt fall into two stylistic groups, and the discovery that each group has different trace elements provides clear evidence that they were made at different mints.

Attributing coins to mints

Once coins have been classified into groups, the next stage is to determine the exact date of a coin's manufacture or the precise location of its mint. These are separate problems and require different methods.

Coins quite frequently indicate their place of minting. This is normally the case with the coinages of ancient Greece or medieval England: the coins have inscriptions such as the Greek 'Athe' (short for 'Athenaion', 'of Athens') (fig. 9) or the medieval Latin 'CIVITAS LONDON'('the city of London') (figs. 3 and 5). In the same way a late Roman coin might have the mint mark LON standing for Londinium, the short-lived Roman mint at London which operated between AD 286 and 326. But often there is no such indication of mint, or indeed such indications may be misleading: many imitative Athenian coins were minted in Egypt during the fourth century BC with the same designs and inscription as genuine Athenian coins, and the Scandinavian coins with English 'mint names' have already been mentioned (see p. 18).

In these cases the most useful and straightforward method of determining the mint is to study the location of find spots or provenances. Coins are generally found in the same region as their mint, since the function of a mint was usually to supply that region with coinage. For instance, the bronze coinage of the Roman Emperor Nero can be classified into two general groups (see fig. 13). One of these is found predominantly in Italy and the other in northern Europe. As we know that there were two mints under Nero, one at Rome and one at Lyon, we can conclude that the northern group was produced at Lyon and the southern group at Rome. To take another example, provenance has also proved a useful method of attributing 'sceattas', the small silver coins which circulated in England during the eighth century. Two types, one with a pecking bird and one with a facing head, have been found in relatively large numbers in the excavations at Southampton and only rarely elsewhere. An attribution to a mint at Hamwic, the medieval precursor of Southampton, therefore seems plausible.

There are, of course, dangers in this sort of procedure. First, the area of circulation of a coin was usually in direct proportion to its value and the scale on which it was minted. Two of the very common gold coins of the Roman Emperor Claudius I, struck from the same dies, have been found in hoards as far apart as Kent and southern India. The method of attribution by provenance works best with coinages of a small scale or a low value, such as bronze coinage. Second, there are cases of coins being made in one place and then transported elsewhere before entering into circulation. One group of the coins of the Roman Emperor Valentinian was minted at Siscia, in modern Yugoslavia, but is found in large numbers in Britain. Similarly, some coins of the Emperor Septimius Severus which were minted at several cities in southern Greece are found, almost exclusively, in the Levant.

But these cases seem to be exceptional and therefore, provided that the potential dangers and difficulties are borne in mind, provenance will normally provide a good indication of mint. Indeed, in the case of the imitations of Anglo-Saxon coins, provenance has indicated that some groups, previously attributed to the mint at Dublin under Sihtric III because of die links with coins bearing these names, were in fact made in Scandinavia, and that the coins of Sihtric were themselves also imitations.

The method of attribution by provenance can also be used in reverse, in cases where we know the name of a mint from the coins but do not know its location. For example, the location of many of the smaller cities in the eastern part of the Roman empire, in Asia Minor, is unknown. But sometimes a site where classical ruins have been found can be identified from the coins found there, since most cities made small amounts of bronze coinage which tended to circulate in their immediate vicinity. A similar approach has been used in the attempt to define the extent of the Celtic kingdoms in Britain during the hundred years before the Roman conquest of AD 43 (fig. 7). During this period coinage was minted throughout southern and especially south-eastern Britain. Over the years an archive of find spots has been collected and distribution maps can be drawn. When the find spots are plotted by king or tribal grouping it is reasonable to infer that the area of circulation of their coins, especially when these are of low value, reflects the territory of a king or tribe. Thus we can assert that the kingdom of Cunobelin (Shakespeare's Cymbeline), whose capital and mint we know was at Camulodonum (Colchester), extended over most of Essex and Hertfordshire.

Dating

The designs or inscriptions of ancient and medieval coins generally tell us rather less about their dates than about their mints. Few Greek coins bear explicit dates, although some of the eras in use in the Hellenistic period appear on coinage, notably on the coinage of the kings of Syria which are regularly dated by the Seleucid era beginning in 312 BC. The only Roman coins to bear an explicit date were some very rare ones made by the Emperor Hadrian in 'the year of the city 874' (i.e., AD 121) and some made by the usurper Pacatian 'in the 1001st year of Eternal Rome' (i.e., AD 249).

Otherwise dates did not appear on western coinage until the thirteenth century. The first dated coin was issued by Valdemar II of Denmark in 1234, but this is an isolated and untypical example, and dates became a frequent part of the design only from the sixteenth century. In Britain the first date appeared on a Scottish gold coin of 1539.

Other sorts of dates do, however, crop up from time to time, namely the regnal year of a particular ruler, such as one of the Ptolemaic kings of Egypt. Regnal years might also appear on coins of the Roman emperors made in the provinces of the empire, while at Rome coins were frequently dated by the

7   The Celtic kingdoms of pre-Roman Britain. We have no direct evidence for the extent of the tribal divisions in the late first century BC and early first century AD. But these have to some extent been inferred from the discrete geographical distribution of each kingdom's coinage. The exact divisions remain uncertain, though it seems clear that rivers such as the Thames could have represented boundaries.

titles of the emperor, such as the tribunician power, which was renewed every year and thus acts as a sort of regnal year. Other titles adopted by rulers give less precise help: for instance, the coins which give Edward III the title 'King of France' were minted after 1337.

Most coins, however, offer no direct evidence for their date, and it is consequently necessary to use other methods for establishing it. Several different methods are available, and each has its own strengths and weaknesses. In each case the idea is to link a point in the sequence or group with a secure chronological fixed point. This fixed point may be almost anything which can be independently dated: another coin, another artefact, a historical event. Such associations are, however, infrequent, since they are usually known to us only by accident. For example, we now know that the gold coins of Persia called 'darics' existed by 500 BC, because a cuneiform document from Persepolis which is dated to the twenty-second year of Darius – i.e., 500 BC – was stamped with the imprint of one such coin.

One is not normally so lucky as to be able to link a coinage so specifically to a historical event or particular date and usually more indirect methods must be used. The principal method is the study of hoards, since coins have frequently been deposited in hoards for safe-keeping and their owners have often been prevented from recovering them for a variety of reasons such as death or forgetfulness. Consequently a relatively large and regular number of hoards have become available for study through their discovery in modern times.

The theory of their study is straightforward. The coins included in a hoard deposited at a given date will all have been made before that date. Very occasionally we are able to date the deposit of a hoard by reference to a historical event, such as the hoard found at Athens in the debris of the Persian destruction of the Acropolis in 480 BC. On other occasions something datable may by chance have been left with the hoard, as with the hoard of gold and silver coins deposited during the English Civil War at Breckenbrough in North Yorkshire; the pot in which the hoards were found also contained two receipts for requisitioned cheese dating to 17 January 1644, so we can be confident that the hoard was deposited in the run-up to the Battle of Marston Moor in July of that year.

More frequently the deposit of a hoard must be dated from coins it contains which are independently datable, if there are any. Such coins may bear the name of a regime or king whose dates are known. Some African coins used to be attributed to the Numidian King Jugurtha (118–105 BC), but the discovery of a hoard at Enna in Sicily in 1966 showed that these coins were actually contemporary with the period of democracy at Syracuse in 214–212 BC, and the coins could therefore be redated and attributed to the Carthaginian expedition against Sicily in 213–210 BC.

It is not, however, very often the case that an individual hoard will contain such easily datable coins. Normally the process of dating by means of hoards is more complicated, and depends on putting together a dossier of several or many hoards (fig. 8). These would probably have been deposited at different times, and the detailed examination of their contents will, in theory, reveal a progression of different parts of a coinage; if one or more of these parts can be attached to an absolute date, it should be possible to estimate a date for the other parts in the progression or sequence. This method has been used with success in the study of the coinage of archaic and classical Greece, where, for instance, the evidence of several large hoards has enabled a fairly detailed sequence and chronology to be established for the earliest Greek silver coins, made in the fifty years or so before about 475 BC. But the most impressive use of the hoard method concerns the coinage of the Roman Republic. This was produced under the supervision of an annually changing board of three moneyers, who placed their names on the coins. By analysing the evidence of many hoards it has been possible to establish the dating of the annual moneyers with a fair degree of accuracy, to within about five to ten years, although the process is by no means complete and new hoards continue to suggest revisions.

	Moneyer	Hoard 1	2	3	4	5	6	7
49 BC	Mn Acilius	×	×	30	26	6		36
48 BC	Hostilius Saserna			9	9	3	×	14
	Vibius Pansa			2	1	1	×	27
	Albinus				1	2	×	20
47 BC	Plautius Plancus					1	×	19
	Licinius Nerva					1	×	5
	Antius Restio					–	×	2
46 BC	Cordius Rufus					6	×	120
	Carisius					1	×	128
	Considius Paetus					2	×	35
45 BC	Papius Celsus						×	4
	Palikanus							
	Valerius Acisculus							

8   Dating by hoards: the occurrence of Roman Republican silver denarii of the 40s BC in seven hoards helps to establish a precise dating for them. This table gives the numbers of each moneyer's coins in each hoard; an x denotes that these are not known for certain. This method has been used with increasing success since the middle of the nineteenth century.

The potential of hoard studies has been realised only over the last century. Previously a much more common method of dating coins was through their style. The use of stylistic criteria for dating coins should, in theory at least, be as valid in the study of coinage as it is in any other field of art history. For example, the analysis of stylistic details of the representation on a coin, such as the treatment of the hair or the eye, and its comparison with the same features in other well-dated art forms such as vase painting or sculpture, should enable a date to be applied to a coin series, particularly in a period of rapid stylistic change in the arts (such as early Greece). In general this is certainly true, as the experienced eye can tell at a glance whether the style of an ancient Greek coin is that of the archaic or of the later, classical period; in a similar way one can argue from the change in the type of helmet worn by the goddess Athena on Athenian vases in the period 540–510 BC that Athenian coins depicting the same goddess with the same helmet are unlikely to have been made before that time. But problems begin to arise when such stylistic criteria are pressed more precisely. This is partly because the comparison of stylistic elements in different media such as vase painting and coinage is not as straightforward as it seems. For instance, in 1936 the style of certain Athenian coins was compared with that of other arts, and the conclusion was drawn that the coins were produced at the same time as the other objects, i.e., 565 BC; but we now believe that the true date of these coins is some sixty years later. There is an additional problem since coin designs might sometimes deliberately avoid the most recent currents in art. The confidence which was necessary for the successful functioning of a coinage tended to encourage a conservative approach to its design, and one of the largest and most abundant coinages of the ancient world, that of Athens in the fifth and fourth centuries BC, deliberately preserved an archaic appearance, as a comparison with more up-to-date treatments of the same subject reveals (fig. **9**).

9 Immobilised designs. The first two coins (*left*) are both Athenian, but one was made in the early fifth century BC and the other in the mid fourth. The deliberate retention of the archaic style can be seen from a comparison with the head of the same deity, Athena, on a coin of Thurii of the late fifth century (*below*).

Thus stylistic dating needs to be used with great care, and it must be accepted that the results it can give are not particularly secure. Indeed, sometimes it is not very useful, as there may have been long periods without any clear artistic developments, such as the Roman empire of the fourth and fifth centuries or the early medieval period.

Other methods of dating coins are useful, though on an even less frequent basis. One of these is the study of the fabric or physical appearance of coins. With the passing of time, Greek silver coins tended to have a wider diameter and lesser thickness, and a glance at the general appearance of a coin will enable it to be assigned to either the fifth to fourth centuries or the second to first centuries BC (compare figs. 9 and 6). A second useful way of dating is through overstrikes, but these occur in only a few instances. An overstrike occurs when one coin is re-struck, generally at a different mint, by another coin (fig. **10**). Sometimes overstriking has not obliterated the original coin or

10 Overstrikes. The coin of Metapontum (*left*), which was minted in the early fifth century BC, was struck over a coin of Corinth (*right*). The mane and the wing of the Corinthian pegasus are visible beneath and to the left of the corn ear of Metapontum.

'undertype' completely, and detailed examination enables both undertype and overtype to be identified. It is then certain that the undertype was minted earlier than the overtype. Thus, for example, the overstriking by cities in southern Italy of coins of Corinth has enabled a definite date of about 335 BC to be established in the sequence of coinage produced at those south Italian mints.

A change in the weight or fineness of a coinage can occasionally provide a link between an undated and a dated coin. Perhaps the best example of this method is offered by the Merovingian gold coinage of the sixth and seventh centuries AD (fig. 11). Most Merovingian coins of the period have inscriptions which refer only to the moneyer and the place of mintage, but there are a very few with a king's name. The gold coinage of the period was suffering a considerable debasement (whereby the alloy progressively consisted of less gold and more silver), and the metal analysis of the royal pieces has allowed the stages of this debasement to be dated. The moneyers' pieces can be dated by a comparison of their alloy with that of the royal issues. A specific consequence is the dating of the famous ship burial at Sutton Hoo to about AD 625, on the basis of the dating of the hoard of Merovingian coins included among the contents.

Very occasionally a group of coin finds can be associated with a historical event such as the destruction of a city or a battle. For example, many coins have been recovered at the battlefield of Alesia (Alise-Sainte-Reine, Côte d'Or, in central France), the site of the decisive battle in 52 BC between Julius Caesar and the coalition of Gallic tribes led by the chieftain Vercingetorix. The excavations carried out by Napoleon III in 1860–5 found 134 Roman coins (the latest of about 54 BC) and 447 coins made by the Celtic tribes of Gaul. The site consequently provides a key to dating and understanding the contemporary Celtic coinage. For instance, coins of the tribe of the Carnutes inscribed with the name 'Yllycci' were present, whereas those with 'Giamilos' were absent; the inference is that the former were produced before 52 BC and the latter after that date. A series of many similar observations can be made for a number of different tribes and issues, and cumulatively these give us a very clear picture of the extensive series of Celtic silver coinages of the first century BC.

Other criteria may also be useful for dating. One such is epigraphy, the comparison of letter forms between coins and dated inscriptions on stone. Imitation is another; this is when one coin imitates another datable coin or other artefact, or vice versa, as in the case of some early Roman coins which were imitated on pottery that can be independently dated to 285–265 BC. A third is archaeological context: very occasionally a coin or group of coins can be dated from the other objects in the same stratum, as revealed by excavation. For example, a hoard of coins from Isthmia in Greece was found deposited in layers associated with the construction of the Temple of Poseidon, and the pottery in these layers is datable to about 480–470 BC.

It is possible to increase the list of criteria and examples almost indefinitely. But it should be clear that while one or two methods may be the most important for attributing coins to a mint or dating them, almost any other consideration can be important, depending on its relevance or on the accidents of survival. It is often the case that one of these methods can be combined with documentary or historical information, or two or more of the methods or approaches can be combined. One of the best examples is provided by the American excavations at the site of Serra Orlando in Sicily. These excavations produced 706 bronze

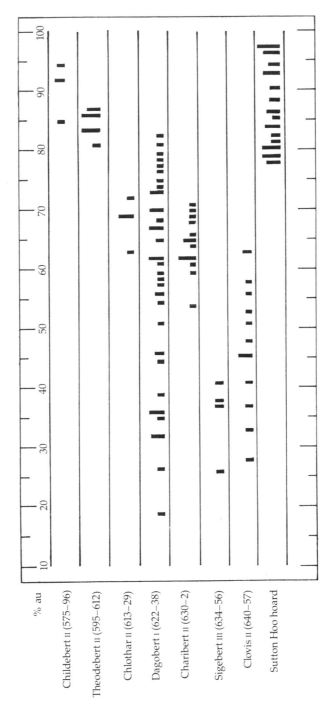

11 The fineness of Merovingian gold. The chronology of the decline of the gold content (% au) can be established by analysing the few coins which bear the names of kings (listed above) and so can be dated. This can be compared with the gold content of the undated coins in the Sutton Hoo burial, and it is apparent that none of them could be later than AD 630. The hoard can therefore be dated to about 625, some thirty years earlier than had previously been thought. The lengths of the bars denote the quantity of coins analysed.

coins inscribed HISPANORUM, which had previously been very rare, and thereby indicated that their mint should be located at Serra Orlando. We happen to know from the historian Livy that a city called Morgantina was settled by the Romans with a group of Spaniards who were fighting on their side in Sicily, after they had captured it from the Carthaginians in 211 BC, and the coins thereby enabled the site to be identified as that of Morgantina. Moreover, the excavations produced much evidence of the destruction of buildings and the massacre of the population, which took place after the successful Roman siege of 211 BC, and among the destruction layers were found a number of the earliest issues of the Roman denarius coinage, whose introduction could thereby be dated to 211 BC or shortly before. As a result, the controversy which had raged for many years about the date of the introduction of the denarius was resolved. In this way coins were dated from the excavation of a site whose identity and history were revealed by other coins.

In the same way that coins with mint names can be used to identify sites, so datable coins can be used to date objects or structures found in association with them. The most obvious case is when a hoard includes both coins and other objects; indeed it is *only* in these cases that the objects in question can be accurately dated (or rather the date by which they must have been made can be accurately established). For example, much of our knowledge of late Roman silverware derives from the great hoard from Kaiseraugst in Switzerland, which included coins that help to date its deposition to AD 350. The same is true for many other periods; for instance, coins provide a date for the deposit of the great Viking hoard from Cuerdale in Lancashire of c. AD 905, and this in turn provides a date for the associated objects and hence a pivotal fixed chronological point for our understanding of Anglo-Saxon metalwork.

— 3 —

The Evidence of Designs

The designs and inscriptions placed on coins played two main and complementary roles, monetary and political. The monetary role enabled the coin to function properly as a coin by ensuring that it circulated smoothly and without interruption. This was achieved through the way that the design referred to the issuing authority. It might include a direct reference to a sovereign ruler or a state, or a more indirect one such as an achievement of the ruler or a symbol of the state's religious life. Such designs encouraged confidence in the acceptance of a coin by appealing to the user's sense of loyalty (whether secular or religious). At the same time they implied a threat of punishment against the user if the coin was abused in some way. Refusal in payment, forgery or any other misuse thereby became treason or sacrilege and attracted savage penalties.

The political role of the coin was manifested in the way that the widespread use of coinage enabled a regime or state to impose its authority in all of the many monetary transactions which take place in any society. This, for instance, is one of the significant points revealed by the story in the Gospel according to St Mark when the Pharisees asked Jesus:

> 'Are or are we not permitted to pay taxes to the Roman emperor? Shall we pay or not?' He saw how crafty their question was, and said, 'Why are you trying to catch me out? Fetch me a silver piece, and let me look at it.' They brought one, and he said to them, 'Whose head is this and whose inscription?' 'Caesar's,' they replied. Then Jesus said, 'Pay Caesar what is due to Caesar, and pay God what is due to God.'

The story reveals how, just as it was taken for granted that God's authority should prevail throughout all life, so the use of Roman coins symbolised how much the Roman emperor's authority prevailed throughout the Roman empire. Coinage was a pervasive symbol of the authority responsible for its issue.

These different roles played by the designs normally existed at a subconscious level, and different societies have attached more weight to one or the other. In medieval Europe and Islam, for example, the monetary stability of the coinage was adjudged paramount and consequently the same design was retained for long periods to maintain public confidence and implicitly offer reassurance about the unchanging quality of the coinage; we have already noted in Chapter 2 the same sort of attitude in Athens during the fifth and fourth centuries BC (see figs. 9 and 3).

At other periods more emphasis might be placed on the political role of the coin design and this allowed a greater variety of designs to be used. In the coinage of the early Roman empire, for example, nearly all coins had the emperor's head on one side, but on the other a great variety of designs were used. In Rome these stressed the emperor's achievements (military victories, public works, etc.), his virtues and divine endorsement of his regime; in the provinces they dwelt on the important cults or monuments of the city which made them.

On very rare occasions the design might even give prominence to the individual moneyer, the man responsible for the coin's manufacture. There was a tendency in the later Greek world or in Merovingian Gaul and Anglo-Saxon or Norman England for the name of the moneyer or responsible official to appear prominently in the legend. But even more remarkable is the case of the Roman Republic, where for a century designs referring to the moneyers completely supplanted the symbols of the state; the moneyers had the freedom to choose their own personal designs, such as family achievements or origins (see fig. 15). A similar state of affairs had existed only at the very dawn of coinage when, in a number of areas including Asia Minor or Athens, a variety of personal designs had appeared, perhaps implying that for a short time after its inception coinage was sometimes produced on the authority of prominent individuals rather than of the state.

A consequence of these different attitudes to and use of coin design was that the designs of some coinages offer a very limited repertoire. Some, such as those of most of the Islamic states, have only inscriptions and no designs, because of their religious rejection of images. Others, such as those of the Graeco-Roman world, offer an almost infinite variety of illustrations; many cases, of course, fall somewhere in between. It is not possible here to give anything like a complete view of what we can learn from coin designs, and the following discussion will only characterise some of the potential and the pitfalls of using them.

The discussion here will be limited in two main ways, in view of the space available. First, it will concentrate on the images on coins rather than the inscriptions. Coin inscriptions do indeed have much to offer. They can tell us about political slogans (see pp. 37–8), and give us important information about the people and places who made them. This information is all the more important because of the official nature of coins, which thereby gives them an advantage over other more private inscriptions. For example, coins provide the fullest and most systematic source for the names and titles of Roman emperors and may sometimes provide the basic framework for the chronology of their reigns. They can also tell us the correct name of a city. Coin inscriptions tell us, for example, that the city of Eumenea in Asia Minor briefly changed its name to Fulvia, in honour of Mark Antony's wife of the same name; this was later regarded as shocking and people tried to erase the name from the coins.

As well as the names of cities, coin inscriptions can tell us much about a city's institutions and individuals. For the Roman period, they provide a wealth of information about the names of festivals and magistracies, as well as the names of the people who held them. The names of moneyers would not otherwise be known; from them we can reconstruct the careers of Roman politicians. For a later period, the coins demonstrate that many of the same men were moneyers before and after the Norman conquest of England in 1066, and so are a vivid sign of administrative continuity between late Anglo-Saxon and early Norman England.

The sort of information, however, which can be gleaned from coin inscriptions is much like that derived from inscriptions on other media. But while the large number of coins means that they give us a large quantity of information, their small size and the consequent brevity of their inscriptions greatly restricts the level of interpretation we can make from them compared with, say, a lengthy edict of a Roman emperor fully inscribed on stone.

The second limitation of this discussion is that it will concentrate on the Graeco-Roman world, as this was a period when coin designs were at their most varied. The choice to concentrate on this period should not be taken as implying that coin designs are unimportant in the study of other cultures, for this is not at all the case. For the purposes of this book, however, the wealth and variety of different designs on Greek and Roman coins give the greatest opportunities and indeed difficulties of interpretation.

The discussion will fall into two parts: an examination, first, of the sort of information that can be gleaned from a study of individual coins, and, second, of how the study of groups of coins can throw light on contemporary propaganda.

Individual coins

Greek and Roman coinages provide information about almost every aspect of classical civilisation. The inscriptions give information about the titles of emperors and cities or the names of individuals responsible for the coinage. The designs show games in the circus or gladiatorial shows; aspects of political life, such as voting; the natural world (animals, fish, trees, insects); warfare (depictions of soldiers and weapons); religion (temples, cult scenes, gods, mythology); and daily life (ordinary objects of everyday existence). Two are discussed here: representations of buildings, and portraits.

Architecture

Coins are one of our most fruitful sources of information for the appearance of ancient buildings. They are depicted on coins particularly of the period of the Roman empire, and especially for the two hundred years between AD 50 and 250. Almost a thousand buildings are represented, mainly from the city of Rome and from eastern provinces of the Roman empire. Many of these are temples, but there are also fountains, lighthouses, bridges, aqueducts, arches, gates and city walls. Relatively few Roman buildings have survived in anything like a complete state, and coins therefore offer an unrivalled source of information regarding the appearance of ancient cities, as well as an invaluable tool for archaeologists in their efforts to reconstruct classical buildings from those remains which may survive.

But the evidence of coins is not as straightforward as it might seem. This can be illustrated by taking two extreme cases. On the one hand, coins can give us the only information we have about some buildings, such as the vanished Roman Temple of Augustus and Livia between the Palatine and Capitol which was restored by Antoninus Pius in AD 158–9. At the other extreme, coins occasionally depict buildings which were never built, such as the Temple of the Clemency of Caesar on coins of 44 BC, or the round Temple of Mars Ultor on coins of 19 BC. The latter was not finished until 2 BC and in the end bore no resemblance to the structure on the coins. In this case the coin artist was presumably commemorating the decision to build the temple.

In other ways, too, the evidence of coins needs to be used with sensitivity, since the depictions on coins are not at all like modern photographs. It would be wrong to suppose that a depiction on a coin is an exact reproduction of an ancient building, as this is to misunderstand the intentions of the die engraver. His intention was to convey the significant or important characteristics of a building. For example, the representation of a temple on a coin may show a gap in the middle of the columns which is filled with an image of the relevant god (fig. 12). But no classical temple had such a gap, nor was the cult image visible from outside; it was enclosed by a wall in the sanctuary or cella of the temple. But the gap in the columns showing the cult image is the convention adopted by the die engraver to convey the essential nature of the temple and the identity of its cult, or perhaps to express the epiphany of the god.

Although the depiction of an ancient building on a coin cannot be taken entirely at face value, it would be equally wrong to conclude that the evidence of coins is worthless in reconstructing the architectural history of the ancient world. But it is important to appreciate the sorts of conventions which were adopted by the engravers of coin dies in their attempts to represent three-dimensional structures on a two-dimensional plane. Many of these conventions fall into the categories of abbreviation and omission. So, for instance, a temple with eight columns might be shown on a coin as having eight, six, four or two; it was sufficient to show that it had a columned portico. In the same way a temple which was situated at the top of a flight of steps might be shown on top of steps, though the number of steps on the coin would normally be fewer than in reality. The convention of abbreviation is relatively straightforward, but other conventions are more complicated, such as the above-mentioned depiction of a cult image in a gap in the middle of the columns.

In ways such as this one has to be careful in using coin evidence, but, allowing for these and similar qualifications, it can still be extremely useful. The study of any building shown on coins, however, must be based on a full collection of the available coins. This is partly because the depiction of the same building on coins of a particular city at different dates may, through its variation, reveal complementary details. We can take two examples. The first concerns the appearance of the famous Temple of Diana at Ephesus, one of the Seven Wonders of the Ancient World (fig. 12). We know that its facade had eight columns, and we find coins showing any number from two to eight, but never more. In addition coins have provided decisive evidence for the position in the structure of carved column drums, one of which can be seen today in the British Museum. Early reconstructions of the temple placed these on square pedestals, but it is clear from the coins that the pedestals did not form part of the base of the columns. From various other coins we can see that the pediment had three openings or windows and was decorated with four sculptural figures below a central Medusa head at the apex. None of this architec-

12 The Temple of Diana at Ephesus, on coins of Maximus (AD 235–8) (*top*) and Valerian (AD 253–60).

tural information would otherwise be known. Second, in the case of the lost triumphal Arch of Nero, a careful compilation of the surviving specimens and analysis of the dies represented in them can help establish the fullest and most reliable reconstruction of the monument (fig. **13**).

13 The lost Arch of Nero at Rome, depicted on coins minted at Rome (*top*) and Lyon (*left*) (the coins from Lyon can be distinguished by the small globe at the point of the emperor's neck). The arch shown on the less reliable Lyon coin is shorter and squatter. There are also differences of detail: for example, on the Lyon coin the pedestal under the figure of Mars is missing, and there is no relief sculpture on the attic below the chariot.

Portraiture

Portraiture has been a focus of interest in coins since the Renaissance, for the portraits which had survived on Roman coins provided a profound moral paradigm to Renaissance rulers. For instance, when Petrarch met the Emperor Charles IV at Mantua in 1354 he gave him some Roman coins with the words, 'Look, Caesar, on those whom you have succeeded; look on those you should strive to emulate.' The lesson was not wasted on Renaissance princes, who adopted individual portraiture on their own coins, in the hope that these would survive as lasting memorials to their achievements in the same way as Roman coins had; this adoption of portraiture thereby laid one of the foundations of modern coin design.

Previously, from the time of the late Roman emperors to the late Middle Ages, coins had borne representations of rulers, but these were only generic images of royalty rather than individual portraits. The depictions of the emperor on late Roman gold coins remained unchanged for 150 years from the mid-fourth century (fig. 18), while the appearance of kings on, say, English silver coins were virtually identical for some three centuries, from the reign of Edward I (1272–1307) to that of Henry VII (1485–1509) (figs. 3 and 19). Conversely, the images used on coins of the Anglo-Saxon kings – for example, Edward the Confessor – are greatly varied and inconsistent (unbearded and bearded). For some thousand years there was virtually no attempt to give a ruler an individual image.

Individualised portraits, however, had been produced on coins and other media in large numbers from about 300 BC to AD 350. Portraits had been very infrequent earlier in the classical world, since the ideals of the Greek city-state precluded the glorification of an individual. But this attitude changed from the time of Alexander the Great (336–323 BC) (fig. 14). His conquests transformed the ancient world and ushered in the Hellenistic age of great monarchies. The depiction of individual rulers was appropriate to this new royal order, and in this respect the Roman emperors succeeded to the practice of their Hellenistic predecessors.

14 Alexander the Great (336–323 BC), depicted on a silver coin of his successor, Lysimachus (306–281 BC). He is shown with his eyes and neck turned upwards, and his hair is bound with a diadem (a white cloth), the symbol of royalty.

But while Hellenistic and Roman portraits were individualised, this does not mean that they were necessarily realistic. Sometimes they demonstrably were not; for example, portraits of the Emperor Augustus struck at the end of his reign, when he was seventy-six, do not depict a man of that age and do not correspond with the unflattering description given by his biographer, Suetonius. Portraits such as this are intended to be the embodiment of a political ideal rather than a realistic likeness (though in some cases, such as that of Nero, they might be both).

The study of portraits on coins is therefore as much about the political factors that influenced them as about their intrinsic or moral interest. And, as the political factors which influenced the appearance of coin portraits, generally speaking, had a similar effect on portraits in other media, we can use coins in many ways in the study of ancient portraiture. Coins can make three contributions to this study, all of which derive from the way that coin portraits are normally identified by the inscription that accompanies them and from the fact that they have survived in much greater numbers than have portraits in any other medium.

15 Silver denarius of the Roman Republican moneyer C Antius Restio (c. 47 BC), with a portrait of his father, tribune in 68 BC. It illustrates the great freedom which the moneyers were allowed in the choice of design. Restio's father's portrait belongs to a different tradition from that in vogue in the Hellenistic world (contrast fig. 14; compare fig. 16).

In the first place, coins can supply portraits of persons for whom we have no other likeness. Portraits of the famous Roman emperors are known from a large number of other sources, principally sculpture, but for many of the Hellenistic kings or Roman emperors of the third century AD, coins provide the only portrait evidence. The extent of the 'gap' thereby filled by coin evidence can be appreciated from a glance at any book on Hellenistic or Roman portraiture. Sometimes coins even give us portraits of members of the imperial family who are otherwise unattested: the Emperor Uranius Antoninus (a usurper in Syria in AD 253–4); Dryantilla, the wife of Regalian (c. AD 260); or Cornelia Supera, the wife of Aemilian (AD 253). An example of the political interpretation of coin portraiture can be seen in the fine portraits of a certain Tarcondimotus, who was appointed by the Romans to be the ruler of a small part of south-east Asia Minor in the late first century BC, and subsequently given the title 'king' by Mark Antony. As an expression of his political allegiances, his portrait is therefore rendered in the Roman rather than the Hellenistic tradition, and shows the influence of the portrait of his patron Antony – for instance, in the treatment of the nose, mouth and chin (fig. 16).

16 Bronze coin of Tarcondimotus, King of Cilicia (south-east Asia Minor), late first century BC. The portrait of the king belongs to the Roman rather than the Hellenistic tradition (compare fig. 15; contrast fig. 14).

A second role of coins in the study of portraiture lies in the help that they may give in the identification of other portraits, particularly sculptures, since it is only very rarely that the latter's accompanying inscriptions have survived to identify them. Many of the identifications of portraits of Roman emperors which nowadays seem self-evident do in fact ultimately depend on the associations made by scholars since the Renaissance between these portraits and labelled coins. These have been possible because the portraits of Roman emperors of the first two centuries AD were, for the most part, strongly individualised and because portraits in the round have survived in large numbers – there are in some cases well over a hundred examples for each emperor.

But identification is more difficult when relatively few portraits in the round have survived. We can see from their coins that the portraits of Roman emperors of the third century AD were individualised, but the identification of their three-dimensional portraits is still difficult because not many survive (a result in part, at least, of the very short life expectancy of an emperor during this troubled period).

Problems of identification also arise when portraits are less individualised, as in the case of the immediate successors of the Roman Emperor Augustus, who modelled their portraits on the founder of their dynasty. But the problems are offset by the relatively large number of (marble) portraits which have survived, thus facilitating their classification and identification.

In some cases, difficulties arise because of a combination of less individualisation and low survival. The Hellenistic kings tried to provide a visual legitimisation of their position by choosing portraits which were closely derived from those of Alexander the Great. Moreover, not very many of their sculptural portraits have survived (only a few over a hundred for the three centuries after Alexander), partly because they were often made of bronze which was readily melted down for re-use.

Cases of problematic identification may often be just as revealing as cases where it is easier, since they raise political questions of why, at certain periods, portraits were more individualised or sculptural portraits were rare.

The third main contribution of coins to the study of portraits is to their chronology. Because coins were mass-produced they can often be accurately dated, in the ways described in Chapter 2. So in the case of a ruler who reigned for a long time, coins enable us to date the changes during the reign. A good example is Augustus, who changed his type of portrait in response to his changing political circumstances (see also p. 39), and these changes can be approximately dated from coins (fig. 17). In the case of the Emperor Nero, we can tell from coins that he abandoned his youthful hairstyle for the more mature one 'arranged in steps' (as Suetonius calls it) in AD 63 (fig. 13). This hairstyle is modelled on that of actors and musicians, and is derived from that on statues of Apollo as the lyre-player. Nero's adoption of this type of official portrait was an aspect of his revival of the practice of likening the emperor to a god, a practice which had been avoided by the emperors of the previous ninety years (see also p. 40); at the same time the choice of this particular model

17 Portraits of the Roman Emperor Augustus. The first portrait (*top left*) was made at the beginning of his reign, in about 30 BC, and is derived from Hellenistic royal models (compare fig. 14). The second (*lower left*) was made in the very last year of the reign, AD 14; although it is a different type of portrait, it hardly represents Augustus as a man aged seventy-six.

18 Ruler images of the late Roman and early Byzantine empires. The top coin has a representation of the Emperor Constantius II (AD 337–61), the lower one of Anastasius (AD 491–518). The similarity of the 'portraits' illustrates the lack of importance attached to the individualisation of the emperor's image.

marks a major stage in the growing importance Nero attached to his own theatrical and musical performances which, when given in public, deeply shocked traditional Romans.

19 Royal images of the late English Middle Ages. The top coin shows Henry VII (1485–1509); it is the same generic royal image which had been used for two centuries, as can be seen from the close similarity of the image used by Edward I (compare fig. 3). But with the Renaissance there was a return to the individualised portraits of antiquity, as can be seen in the portrait of the next king, Henry VIII.

Propaganda and groups of coins

A second way of approaching coin designs is to look at groups of designs. The examination of all the images produced during a particular period or of a selection of images over a longer period will often provide a good idea of how the relevant state or regime wished to represent itself. Self-representation in this way was never as systematically developed as the products of modern propaganda machines, but, as with the study of portraiture, it can be very revealing about the aspirations and claims of any regime, matters which are as interesting to the historian as the reality of what actually happened.

The use of political symbols on coins naturally becomes particularly strident at times of crisis, especially during periods of civil war. For example, it may come as something of a surprise to find that, during the English Civil War, the Parliamentarian party, which controlled London and the mint in the Tower, emphasised its legitimacy by continuing to issue coinage in the king's name, whereas at the Royalist mint of Oxford the king's coinage proclaims: 'RELIG PROT LEG ANG LIBER PAR' ('The religion of the Protestants, the laws of

England and the liberty of Parliament'). Coins could play a similarly important propaganda role at other periods of civil war, particularly in the Roman world, when the designs on coins were constantly changing. The 'year of the four emperors' took place in AD 68–9, when after the death of Nero no less than four individuals wore the purple: Galba, Otho, Vitellius and the eventual winner, Vespasian. During these months the messages conveyed by coinage became very simple and explicit. Galba's coinage proclaimed the 'Concord of the Provinces', the 'Rebirth of Rome', the 'Restoration of Liberty' and even the 'Preservation of the Human Race' under his rule; Otho's proclaimed 'Peace in the World' or the 'Safety of the Roman People', while Vitellius's emphasised the 'Loyalty of the Army', the 'Concord of the Roman People' and of course the 'Restoration of Liberty'; and the same dies blazoning these claims were coupled with obverse dies for three different emperors.

The iconography of a state's coinage viewed over a period of time can reveal a certain amount of information about the aspirations of that state, since the choice of designs will normally reflect the matters considered important by at least an influential body in that state and will present these important matters in a particular way. In the modern world, for instance, one might look at the development of the personification of Britannia as an index of the growing imperialism of Britain (fig. 20). We are, of course, familiar with a heavily armed Britannia brandishing a trident and ruling the waves, but her development in this way is simply an indication of Britain's preoccupation with military conquest since the seventeenth century. There is no *a priori* reason why she should have been modelled on the warlike goddess Minerva (or Roma); indeed, on an Italian medal made in 1564, Anglia (as she then was, before the unification of the kingdoms) appears as a simple female figure dressed in the ordinary clothes of daily life. Her warlike appearance dates only from the next century and is very much a creation of the Restoration court, where she was developed

20 Britannia through the ages. The farthing of 1672 (*top*), minted under Charles II, shows an early armed representation of Britannia. By the time of the farthing of George IV, of 1826, the image had become more warlike with the addition of the helmet and the trident, the latter symbolising Britain's claim to rule the sea.

as a symbol of the victory of the British in the Dutch Wars. Frances Stuart, Duchess of Richmond and the king's mistress, appeared in court masques as Britannia; the subject was taken up by painters including Lely and appeared on contemporary medals and coinage. Her iconography remained more or less constant for over a century until the period of the Napoleonic Wars, at the end of the eighteenth century. It is at this time that the trident became a regular part of her iconography, specifically after the great victory of the Earl of Howe at the battle of the Glorious First of June in 1794; shortly thereafter, from the early nineteenth century, she is also regularly shown as wearing a helmet. It does not take much imagination to see these changes as a reflection of Britain's growing military self-assertiveness, and specifically of her claim to Neptune's trident and rule of the sea.

Similarly, we can look at the iconography of coins over a shorter period. This is a particularly fruitful exercise when there is little contemporary written history. An example is provided by Rome in the late fourth and third centuries BC, the period which saw Rome emerge from being just one of the cities in Italy to become the conqueror of Carthage and a principal power in the ancient world. This new position was achieved only as a result of continuous warfare; there was hardly a year in the third century that did not see the Roman army engaged in some campaign. There has, however, been some debate in modern times about the motivation which lay behind this huge increase in Rome's power: was it the constant aggression of neighbouring states which prompted Rome to take protective measures, and thereby incidentally achieve this new position, or was Rome an imperialist power whose expansion was internally motivated (for example, by land hunger or aristocratic avarice for glory)? The second alternative is supported to some extent by the coinage. The changing designs used on the coinage concentrate on warlike themes – military symbols, gods of war, figures of Victory – and especially symbols borrowed from the iconography of the conqueror *par excellence*, Alexander the Great. His seal ring appears on one coin, while others depict the goddess Roma wearing his war helmet and the god Hercules, who is shown wearing Alexander's diadem and with his hairstyle (fig. **21**). The coins show that contemporary Romans kept returning to the iconography not just of war, but of conquest, and that they presented themselves as following in the footsteps of Alexander; this is an important contribution to our understanding of their aspirations at the time.

21   Rome in the third century BC. The coin depicts Romulus and Remus, the legendary founders of Rome, with the she-wolf which suckled them. The head can be identified as that of Hercules from the club around his neck, but it is a very unusual representation of Hercules: the absence of a beard, the diadem, the upturned eye and the hairstyle are all derived from that of the great conqueror Alexander the Great (compare fig. 14).

We can use the same approach to examine the self-representation of a particular ruler, taking again the example of a Roman emperor such as Augustus (31 BC–AD 14) or Nero (AD 54–68). The first reigned during a period of complex political change, and presided over the difficult transition from the Roman Republic and the civil wars which brought it to an end to the monarchical system which became the Roman empire; Nero's reign marks the abandonment of the pattern which had been established by Augustus. In the case of Augustus we are lucky enough to have the text of *The Achievements of the Divine Augustus*, which was inscribed on public buildings all over the Roman world and may have been written by Augustus himself during the course of his reign. It is perhaps no surprise that there is a close correspondence between the themes announced in *The Achievements* and on the Augustan coinage: his restoration of the Republican constitution, his new name 'Augustus', his personal subventions to the public treasury, his repair of roads and building of temples, his restoration of military standards from Spain, Gaul and Parthia. More subtle are the changes embodied in his own self-representation. His portrait was modified, in stages which can be dated by coins, from a depiction in the tradition of a Hellenistic king to one based on the canons valued in the Greek city-state, thereby reflecting his change from being one of the warlords in the civil wars after Caesar's death to a new 'democratic' position after the settlement as first citizen, 'first among equals' (fig. 17). At the same time the divine symbols which had accompanied his image, such as the thunderbolt of Jupiter or laurel wreath of Apollo, were dropped; throughout his reign Augustus was presented on his coinage, a medium of mass circulation, as a human being (fig. **22**). In such ways Augustus changed his image to match the changing political regime over which he presided. His changes lasted until Nero abandoned the Augustan type of portrait and re-adopted divine symbols; Nero's new hairstyle has already been discussed (p. 36), and he is sometimes depicted at Rome and in the pro-

22 Divine and human representations of the emperor. Both commemorate the same scene: the reception by the Emperor Augustus of a victory won by Tiberius and Drusus in 15 BC.
On the coin the emperor is shown wearing a toga and seated on a chair, receiving the laurel branches of victory. On the decorated sword scabbard he is depicted, like the god Jupiter, half-nude and on a throne. Such divine imagery was confined to extravagant and luxury items such as ornate scabbards and cameos, which were intended for members of the imperial court, and does not appear on objects of mass circulation such as coins, on which representations of Augustus were always human after 27 BC.

vinces wearing the radiate crown, a symbol of divinity, and the aegis, the attribute of Jupiter. Augustus, the 'first among equals', had become Nero, the 'first without equals': the man who had promised at his succession to model his rule on that of Augustus later boasted of his uniqueness and superiority over his predecessors.

In ways such as these coinage was used for contemporary propaganda. The above examples indicate how an examination of a society's or ruler's coins can tell us something about its self-expression and aspirations. The same is true, in addition, of some of the examples considered in the first part of this chapter: the cities of the Roman empire valued the important temples and buildings in their city rather more than, say, the sources of their agricultural wealth or their other important industries such as marble quarries, pottery or metalworking.

Coin designs can reveal much about the past. They can be studied in many different ways and with varying degrees of sophistication. The opportunities they offered to die engravers were limited by their small format and two-dimensionality, which caused difficulties and led to the adoption of some of the conventions that, as we have seen, can sometimes make their interpretation difficult. But these limitations are more than offset by the sheer quantity of coins and hence of the designs made. The durability of coins has ensured the survival of these images from poorly documented periods and has thereby provided, as was realised in the Renaissance, a unique memorial to the achievements and history of the past.

— 4 —

The Economic Evidence

Coins of all periods and cultures behave in similar ways as economic objects, and we can therefore apply the same methods of economic study to all of them. The sort of questions which can be asked concern both the role of coins themselves and the wider implications they may have for an understanding of a particular society. Why were coins made? How were they used? What can they tell us about the nature of an economy? Can we use them to gain knowledge about the size or scale of a state's economy?

The attempt to answer such questions from an examination of the coin evidence is only worthwhile where documentary evidence is deficient. No historian, for instance, would study the economy of a modern society by an examination of its coins (or banknotes); even questions about the way coins are used are usually better answered from anecdotal evidence. When documentary sources exist but are not fully informative, however, we can sometimes supplement them with a study of the coins. For the ancient and medieval worlds documentary information of this type is almost totally lacking, and in the attempt to fill the gap we must turn to coins. A consequence is that the kind of information we can glean is strictly limited – compared, at any rate, with that available for well-documented modern societies – but the results are still sufficiently significant to justify the effort.

There are two basic ways of approaching coin evidence from the economic point of view. The first is an examination of the coins themselves which survive in museums around the world. The second is by looking at the patterns of coin finds, both those revealed by coins deposited in hoards and those which were casually lost and have been recovered in modern times by chance, by treasure hunting or by archaeological excavation. While the methods of study vary with the type of evidence, it will become apparent that different kinds of evidence and methods can frequently be combined, often with the most fruitful results.

Examination of the coins themselves

Weight and fineness of alloy
First and most basically we can look at the physical nature of the coins of any given period, as the study of the amount of silver or gold bullion in a

coin may reveal some historical information. We can gauge the metal composition by establishing its weight and the purity of its alloy, as discussed in Chapter 2. If we find a sudden or gradual drop in weight or fineness, this would appear to indicate a short-term or chronic shortage of bullion and consequently a financial crisis. An example of a short-term crisis reflected in coinage occurred in Rome during the Second Punic War (218–201 BC). The invasion of Italy by Hannibal precipitated a series of military disasters on Rome and had a clear effect on her coinage: the purity of the silver was reduced; the weight standard of the bronze coinage fell away from a standard of 135 g to one of only 54 g; and a coinage of gold was issued (before the Roman imperial period, gold coinage was unusual and generally produced only in times of emergency or crisis). These changes show how financial pressures brought about the collapse of the early Roman coinage system; so much so that it seems that for a time the Roman state had to fight the war on credit given by some of its citizens.

An example of a long-term debasement is provided by the coinage of Rome in the third century AD. The Roman empire saw the increasing debasement of its staple silver coin: from almost pure silver in the early first century AD it sank to only 50 per cent fine by about AD 200 and to only about 1–2 per cent by AD 270. At the same time the weight of the gold coin declined, the scale of its production was greatly reduced, and, at the end of the period, it too was debased so that it was only 70–80 per cent pure. This shows that the gold and silver available to the Roman state was quite inadequate to meet the need for coinage, and that expenditure greatly outstripped income. The causes of this are not entirely clear, but were probably a combination of the increasing costs of warfare (as the empire came under severe pressure from the barbarians across the Rhine and Danube, and from the Persians in the east) and of the exhaustion of the Roman mines in Spain, which seem for the first two centuries AD to have provided an important contribution to the difference between Rome's income (taxes) and expenditure (especially on war).

In the same way the debasement of the gold coinage of the Byzantine empire in the eleventh century – after six centuries of purity – is indicative of a mismatch between resources and expenditure. The fineness of the gold began a gentle decline through the tenth century to about 90 per cent, and debasement accelerated during the following century until it took a sudden nosedive in the two decades between 1071 and 1092, falling from about 70 per cent to a mere 10 per cent. This debasement resulted from imperial extravagance and the catastrophic loss of Asia Minor. We know from a contemporary historian that, under Nicephorus III, 'expenditure exceeded revenue by several times. And so for this reason, cash quickly became lacking, [and] the gold coin was debased.'

But while it is true that an economic or financial crisis will generally have a clear effect on a state's coinage, the converse is not necessarily true: a debasement of the coinage does not in itself indicate a financial crisis, since it might take place for some other reason. Three examples illustrate some of the possibilities.

First, an examination of the gold coinage of Henry VIII would reveal that he introduced a new gold coin with a lower fineness and weight. The motivation was not, however, the difficulty of financing his wars or some other shortage of resources, but was related to the continuing importation of French and

Flemish gold coins into England. These coins contained less gold than English gold coins and, on the principle of 'bad money drives out good', had tended to drain England of its finer gold; this was exported to the continent where it was worth more. In 1526 Wolsey was authorised to make such changes as were necessary to bring English coinage into equality with the principal continental currencies, and coins on the new standard were therefore issued.

Second, a number of states in the Hellenistic period reduced the weight of their coinage. This occurred in Egypt and Asia, for instance, and the intention was to create a closed currency system whereby everyone entering the kingdom had to change their foreign coin into local coin and did not take the local coinage out of the country. This was achieved by a reduction in the weight: within the country a coin with a silver value of three drachmas was officially valued at four, and clearly no one would export it or they would lose 25 per cent of its value. The motive for this system was the provision of income for the royal treasury from the fees charged on the transaction of money-changing; it was not prompted by any financial crisis.

Third, debasement of early medieval coinage in western Europe and the eventual replacement of gold by silver can be attributed to the cessation of the flow of gold bullion from east to west with the abandonment of gold subsidies paid by the Byzantine empire to the barbarians in the west. Moreover, the relative value of gold to silver was much lower in western Europe than it was further east, in the Byzantine and Islamic worlds, so gold tended to leave western Europe and silver became the principal medium for coinage.

The range of denominations
A second way of looking at coins is to examine the denominations in which they were made. On a number of occasions we can note that only coins of a relatively high denomination were minted and hence available for use. Good examples are provided by the earliest phase of Greek silver coinage, when large silver denominations tended to predominate. Some states made small denominations at this date, but these were not common and there was no regular supply. Moreover, the smallest denominations to be produced in any quantity, the silver obol and electrum $\frac{1}{96}$-stater (about the same value as a silver obol), were too valuable for the everyday needs of retail trade. A similar state of affairs obtained for the coinages of Sasanian Persia and medieval England, neither of which issued any significant copper coinage or small silver coins in any quantity. This absence of small denominations would clearly limit the extent to which coinage could have been used. It obviously precluded its use in everyday transactions, such as buying loaves of bread. We can therefore conclude that in these societies a different system of exchange or barter was used for basic daily transactions.

Coins were sufficient, however, for the needs of everyday life in many other ancient societies – for instance, the Hellenistic world or the Roman empire. The range of coins available was sufficient for even the smallest transactions, and we can glimpse from reading a Latin novel such as *The Golden Ass* of Apuleius or from the many papyri which have survived from Egypt that these societies used coinage very much as we do. This picture is confirmed by the large numbers of bronze coins recovered from excavations in ancient cities such as Athens or Rome, which indicate that low-value coins were widely available.

The examination of archaeological evidence can, though, sometimes modify such a view. In Britain during the early Roman empire the smallest denominations are almost completely absent and coinage generally seems to have been less widely available than in other parts of the empire (see p. 51). The conclusion can be drawn that Roman Britain did not attain the same degree of monetisation as the Mediterranean cities.

Estimating the size of a coinage
A third main method of looking at coins is rather more detailed. It consists of trying to estimate the size of a coinage by calculating the number of dies made to produce it. The idea of this method is very simple: to work out the number of dies used for any given coinage and multiply this total by the average number of coins each die could produce. The resulting figure will give the quantity of bullion minted, and this figure will in turn allow some attempt to quantify the cash element of state budgets and to approach questions of money supply (and so, possibly, liquidity).

But if the idea of this procedure is simple, the practice is much less so because of the problems involved. The first stage is to gather as large a sample of coins as possible by assembling a collection of plaster casts or photographs of specimens in the world's principal museums, together with other specimens which may have been illustrated in numerous auction catalogues or hoard publications. Examination of this material (very much as described in Chapter 2) enables the identification of the dies used in the sample, and one can then work out the total number of dies represented in the sample of a given size.

The second stage is to use this figure (of so many dies in a sample of so many coins) to calculate the total likely number of dies which were originally made. Again, the theory of this is straightforward; it is based on standard probability theory, such as is widely used in other disciplines, notably in the biological sciences, where the sampling of a population is an accepted way of establishing the variety of species in a given area.

The detailed argumentation of this stage involves a knowledge of statistics, but different methods have been developed. Some are based on the total number of dies observed in the sample. Some are based on the number of dies occurring with only one specimen, the number with two, the number with three, and so on. Another method plots the progress of the die-studier on a graph. The axes of the graph are the number of specimens and the number of dies. The graph line will at first rise steeply but then start to level off, and one can compute the likely final level and hence the number of dies.

The likely total number of dies can then be multiplied by the average number of coins per die. Here again, however, difficult practical problems may be encountered, since we do not know exactly how many dies a coin die could make. We can, however, establish the correct order of magnitude from a number of sources. The coinage of the Amphictions at Delphi in the late fourth century BC was struck from a quantity of bullion whose approximate size is known from an inscription. In this case we can calculate that the average output per obverse die must have been between 23,000 and 47,000. Second, we can try modern experiments. One such experiment saw three reverse dies make 116, 1490 and 7786 coins before breaking; the obverse die was still usable after all 9392. Third, we can use comparative information. For example, for the reign of Edward I we know, from documentary sources, how much coinage was minted and how many dies were made (fig. 23).

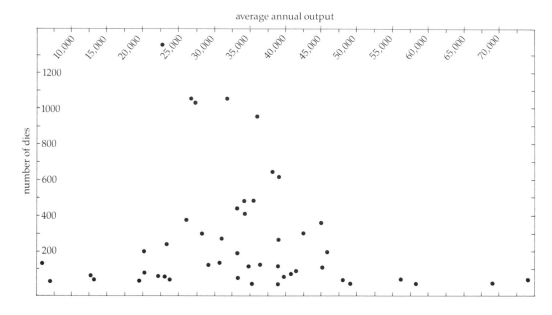

23 The average output of dies. For most of the period 1279 to 1327, we have documentary evidence for the numbers of dies made and coinage struck at the mints of London and Canterbury. On this graph each value represents the average output of a year, calculated by dividing the number of coins by the number of dies. It can be seen that there is a wide variation, especially where the number of dies in a year is small. Note that the average is surprisingly low for the year 1300 (at the top of the graph); but in this year we know of complaints from the king that the dies were of poor quality and made of soft metal.

There are difficulties in interpreting these figures. The Amphictionic coinage, for instance, was made from only a few (nine) dies and may not be typical. The experiments were short-lasting; and we don't know how much we can apply figures from medieval England, with small dies of low relief, to the ancient world. But, despite these uncertainties, there is a general consistency in the figures arrived at from these (and some other) sources which justify us in regarding the average output per die as in the low tens of thousands, and a figure of about 30,000 seems a good working hypothesis.

We can usefully compare figures of output for individual issues, calculated as described above, with records (where they exist) of the amount of money in a state's economy. For example, in the case of Rome in the third century BC, we can calculate that the total amount of silver coinage produced was small in comparison with Rome's 'income' at the time, as defined by plunder, tribute and indemnities, and we can thereby see that silver coinage played only a minor role in the economy. In a similar way we can use the die figures for the early imperial bronze coinages minted at Corinth to calculate that the total value coined over a century was only about half a million denarii, or less than 5000 per year. This is not a large sum and clearly affects our attitude to the function of this and other city coinages produced in the provinces of the Roman empire. Given that the annual cost of a Roman legion was 1.25 million denarii, this calculation shows that provincial bronze coinage is not likely to have been used to pay the wages of Roman legionaries.

46

In more general ways these figures have been used to characterise the liquidity of different periods. For instance, a study of the dies used for the bronze coinage of Antoninus Pius (AD 138–61) circulating in Britain has suggested that the total stock of bronze coinage in circulation was of the general magnitude of about ten million sestertii; as the population of the province was about five million at the time, we can conclude from the low figure of two sestertii per capita that most of the population cannot have used coinage on anything like the scale required in a fully monetised society (see also p. 51). In a rather different way, the estimation of the annual output of the Roman mint between about 150 and 50 BC has enabled a picture to be constructed of the growth and then contraction of the liquidity of silver coinage during that period (fig. 24). This model contains many assumptions and difficulties and may not actually be correct; but this reflects practical problems in the application of the method rather than theoretical flaws in the validity of the approach.

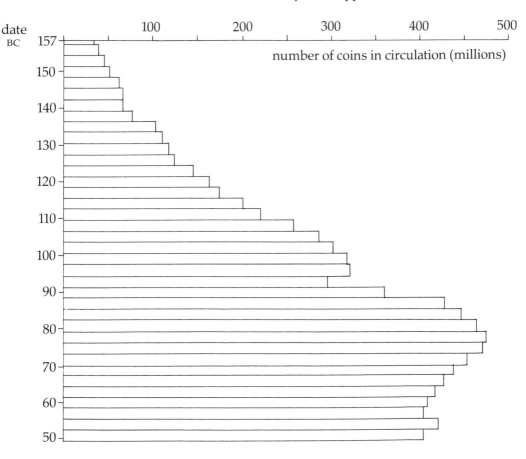

number of coins in circulation (millions)

24 The hypothetical growth and decline of Roman liquidity in the second and first centuries BC. This graph has been constructed by adding the calculated output of each year to the previous total, less a compounded deduction of 2 per cent for each year's loss from circulation. Complaints about a shortage of coins occur in Cicero's letters of the early 40s BC, just when the graph suggests a reduction of liquidity. However, the basis for drawing the graph depends on many uncertainties and is very fragile, and while it shows the potential contribution of die studies and studies of output to our understanding of ancient economies, it is far from certain that it is historically accurate.

Coin finds

The finding of individual coins or of coin hoards can in some rather obvious respects give us the same sort of information, since the loss of a single coin or the deposit of a hoard is proof of some sort of direct or indirect contact between the place of mint and the place of deposit. The discovery of Italian bronze coins of the third century BC in the area of modern Yugoslavia may perhaps indicate the presence there of individual pilgrims, tourists, soldiers or traders from Italy, in much the same way that the presence of hundreds of thousands of Islamic silver coins in Viking hoards of the eighth to tenth centuries is a reflection of the eastward penetration of Viking traders, who exchanged objects such as furs, slaves and amber for silver coinage. But the ways in which coins function as hoards or as individual finds are very different and hence require different approaches, although certain common features, such as the need to establish normal patterns, will be obvious in both.

Individual coin finds
We can examine individual finds or groups of them in different ways, depending on how the find was made, the area in which it occurred or the problem on which it might throw light. The best type of evidence comes from modern archaeological excavation, as we can then be reasonably sure that all the finds from a particular area have been recovered and their original locations and relationships recorded. The systematic publication of coins from excavations began only in the twentieth century, and one of the most substantial early publications was of the coins recovered during the American excavations at Sardis in Asia Minor. However, this volume, which appeared in 1916, can remind us how techniques of archaeology have changed over this century, since the volume included hardly any of the small and often illegible coins which have been found and published in the more recent (1981) volume of Sardis finds. In this case it is clear that the original excavators included only those coins which they deemed of sufficient importance for publication.

A second source of information may be the holdings of museums which have tried to accumulate coins from their relevant collecting areas. The difficulty with this sort of material is that we often do not know if the coins have been acquired on a random and thus representative basis. Museum curators often do not acquire more than one coin of the same type, and may additionally exercise their own judgement about which coins are worth obtaining. Coins may also be acquired from various sources; local finds or gifts of collectors may give very different pictures. But a study of the Roman coins accumulated over the last century or so in museums has thrown up consistent differences between northern France and Italy, enabling certain conclusions to be drawn about the currencies of those areas.

Coins may also be found and reported on a casual basis by interested members of the public or systematically searched out by treasure hunters with metal detectors. Different sorts of problems arise with the evidence provided in this way. First of all, the coins are not necessarily going to be a representative sample from a particular site, because it is unlikely that the whole find complex will be recovered. A few treasure hunters are also acting illegally (for example, by using a metal detector in Britain on a scheduled ancient monument) and may therefore sometimes conceal the find spot altogether or even falsify one.

But in the areas where archaeologists and treasure hunters have good contacts, much information can and has been recovered. For instance, many sites in Britain have been located, such as those of the early medieval markets and fairs which took place outside settlements at Barham near Ipswich or near Royston in Hertfordshire.

The nature of the evidence about coin finds is of varying quality. But even when the information is thought to be reasonably complete and reliable, there are a number of considerations which have to be taken into account in the interpretation of the coins from any site. In the first place, we cannot say that the coins recovered from a site, whether by excavation or otherwise, represent a cross-section of coins in use on that site, even though it is generally true that coins are dropped in proportion to the amount of times they are handled or passed from hand to hand. Once they have been dropped, various factors would affect their survival until modern times. Some sites may have been cleaned more than others in antiquity. Big coins would be more easily recovered by those who lost them than smaller ones. Valuable coins would naturally be searched for with more energy and so tend to be recovered at a higher rate in ancient times. Site finds therefore tend to under-represent more valuable coins.

Second, only rarely would a coin have been lost at or near the same time when it was made; we must bear in mind how long a particular type of coin is likely to have stayed in circulation. Some coins might remain in circulation for centuries. For instance, English coins of the thirteenth century were still available in the fifteenth, so the loss of one could have taken place at any time during its three centuries of circulation. Roman bronze coins of the early second century BC were still being used in the first century AD, and very little bronze coinage was made between about 150 and 20 BC. Thus the finding of a series of coins terminating in about 150 BC could not be used as evidence that the occupation of a site ceased in about that year, for even if occupation had continued for another hundred years, no other coins would have been available to be used and lost. An obvious corollary is that coins with a long circulation life will have been lost in greater proportions than coins with shorter circulation lifetimes.

The lifetime of coins was indeed sometimes very short as a result of various political or economic factors. For example, coins minted with the name and portrait of the unpopular Roman Emperor Caligula were demonetised after his death in order to obliterate his memory. The discovery of a coin of Caligula will therefore be quite good evidence for its loss during his short reign (AD 37–41). In the same way, the frequent coinage reforms of the late Roman empire or late Anglo-Saxon England made it unlikely that the previous issues survived for very long after the date of the reform. One such reform took place in AD 317, and therefore coins made in the previous decade would not have been available after this date for subsequent use and loss.

Third, we cannot say anything about the nature of an individual site from its coins unless we have a typical pattern of coin loss for comparison. For instance, the excavation of a British site might produce several coins of the second century AD, none from the early third century, and large quantities from the late third and mid to late fourth centuries AD. A superficial consideration might suggest that this site was prosperous in the second century, then in recession in the early third century, only to recover in the late third and

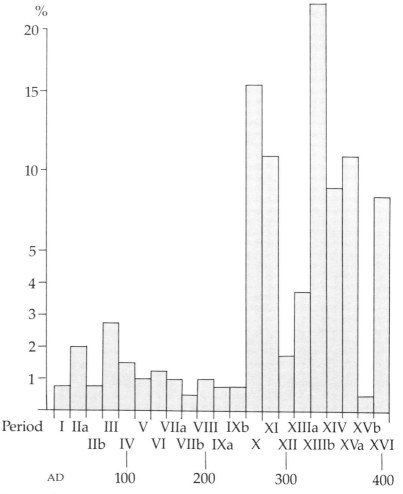

25 The 'typical' pattern of coin loss at a Romano-British site. This pattern has been constructed by finding the mean value of coin loss at eighty-eight sites. For each site the coins were divided up into different periods and expressed as a percentage of the total number of coins recovered. No conclusion can be drawn from the coin loss at any individual site, unless it varies significantly from the pattern.

fourth centuries. But this conclusion would be quite misleading, since the pattern described is typical of all British sites and is a reflection of the coins circulating in Britain throughout its occupation by the Romans (fig. **25**). Only if the coin list from a site varied in some particular way from the typical pattern would we be justified in drawing any specific conclusion about it: an absence of fourth-century coins, say, would strongly suggest that the site was abandoned in that period. Sometimes it is correct to draw such a conclusion from this kind of evidence. For example, the large numbers of coins recovered from the Roman bath at Bath tapered off in number from the middle of the fourth century. This is untypical of British sites. It might, of course, be the case that people stopped throwing good-luck coins into the water for some reason, but, in fact, the coin evidence coincides with archaeological evidence for a cessation of the maintenance of the buildings in the precinct in about AD350, and we can conclude that the religious use of the site tailed off from about that date.

Once a normal pattern has been established, it is easier to say more about sites with abnormal patterns than those conforming to the normal one. In a similar way one can, on a broader scale, compare 'normal' patterns against each other, whether chronologically or geographically. For instance, some sites in Roman Britain have a much greater proportion of third- than of fourth-century coins compared to other sites, and it has been observed that the former tend to be the prestigious settlements of old Roman veteran colonies or tribal capitals, whereas the latter are more likely to be smaller rural sites such as farms, forts or villages. From this it can be inferred that monetary or economic activity (defined as the intensity of coin use and hence loss) was greater in rural than in urban centres in the last century of Roman rule in Britain. In this way coin evidence helps us to distinguish between the nature of different sites and allows us to speculate about their changing roles.

As an example of the geographical comparison of normal patterns we can compare the relative incidence of coins of the first two centuries AD in two different areas such as Britain and Italy. This shows a much smaller proportion of coinage lost (and in use) in Britain than in Italy. Such evidence might be taken to show a much less intense use of coinage in the former than in the latter, a view which could be supported by the calculations based on the material from Bath that very little coinage was available in circulation per capita of the population of Roman Britain (see p. 47). A possible explanation might be that coins were used in the same way as in Italy but by fewer people, namely only those in urban settlements. In turn, this picture could be supported by the comparison of the normal patterns of coin loss for urban and rural sites in the early empire; many rural sites show no appreciable coin loss before the third century. This line of reasoning suggests that in Britain coin use was not generally similar to that in the Mediterranean world of the monetised economy, and that many Romano-British communities retained their pre-Roman 'embedded' economies which were not monetised but depended instead on social and hierarchical relations of redistribution and obligation.

Hoards
The evidence offered by hoards is somewhat different from that of individual finds. There are many different sorts of hoards; two common categorisations are the 'currency' hoard and the 'savings' hoard. A currency hoard is a sum of money put together by drawing all its coins from circulation on a single occasion, whereas a savings hoard is formed by gradually adding coins to a hoard over a period of several years; the difference in the way the coins were collected will affect the internal composition of the hoard. It would, of course, be a mistake to think that all hoards fall into one or other of these categories: they are the opposite ends of a spectrum along which most hoards in reality lie. But the analysis of the composition of a big enough sample should enable a comparison to be made between different hoards and the determination of a 'typical' currency hoard whose contents will most likely represent coins drawn from circulation. This is an area only recently receiving attention, increasingly by using statistical tests for 'normalcy': such studies should bring some objectivity to the assumptions which tend to be made at the moment about the character of individual or groups of hoards.

Such hoards can be studied in two different ways – by an examination of their internal composition, or by consideration of general patterns of hoarding from both the chronological and the geographical point of view.

If we analyse the hoards of a particular region chronologically, it comes as no surprise that the periods with the largest concentration of hoards may often be those of great disruption and upheaval, such as wars. Wars generally prompted the hiding of valuables, and indeed their non-recovery, with the threat or reality of invasion, siege and fighting. An instance is provided by the civil war between Pompey and Caesar in the first century BC, when hoarding was so prevalent that it caused a crisis of liquidity. Other good examples are provided by the Hannibalic War fought between the Romans and Carthaginians under Hannibal in 218–201 BC, and by the English Civil War of 1641–9. Far more hoards have survived from both these relatively short periods than from the immediately preceding or succeeding periods. In the case of the Hannibalic War as many as fifty-four hoards have been found, compared with eighteen for the next whole half-century; in the case of the Civil War there are ninety-eight, compared with twenty-four for the period 1625–41 and nine for 1649–60.

But such patterns of hoarding cannot necessarily be explained simply. The deposition of Roman Republican hoards in Italy does not reflect periods of warfare in that country (fig. 26). Many were, indeed, buried during the Hannibalic War or the civil wars after 49 BC, when much of the fighting took place in Italy, but many other hoards were buried at times during the first century BC when there was no fighting there. In this case the explanation is more indirect: the peaks certainly correspond with periods of warfare, but the wars were fought overseas, mainly in Asia Minor. Large numbers of hoards would have been deposited by Roman legionaries recruited in Italy but prevented (for instance, by death) from returning to recover them.

Nonetheless it remains true that the most common explanation of large numbers of unrecovered hoards is warfare, though in some instances it is believed that economic factors also played a part; in the latter cases a currency or political reform is thought to have rendered the coins worthless and hence the owners would not have bothered to recover them. One such example is the large number of hoards of very debased silver Roman coins hidden in the later third century AD, which comprise coins made just before the currency reforms of that period. Yet it is very hard to believe that this sort of explanation can account for more than a handful of hoards, if any. Comparative evidence from better-documented periods indicates that at times of monetary reform transitional arrangements were made to enable people to exchange their old coins for the new ones. A loss might be made on this transaction, but such a loss would be preferable to the total abandonment of one's savings or wealth, which would in any case have still had a value as bullion. The same is true in cases where coins have ceased to be legal tender because of a change of political regime. We know, for instance, from Pepys' *Diary* that it continued to be possible to exchange coins of the Commonwealth for three months after their demonetisation by Charles II. Thus, in the case of the Roman hoards of the late third century, we should perhaps look for some other explanation. Warfare provides one, although we know very little of the period. A further reason for the apparently high numbers of these hoards could be that, since the coins of this era were very debased, hoards tended to be very large: hoards of 3000 pieces are typical and some as large as 50,000 have been recorded. It is more likely that such hoards will be found today simply because of their size, so we may be dealing with a higher rate of recovery for these hoards than is normal for hoards of other periods.

The second way of looking at the distribution of coin hoards is to plot their geographical positions on a map. This can reveal information of various kinds. It may give evidence of trade, since coins were used as objects of trade. Archaic Greek coins are found in hoards from Egypt and the Levant, as they were exchanged for goods, perhaps grain or slaves; many hoards of Roman silver and gold coins are known from southern India because they were exchanged for luxury items such as exotic spices and perfumes, rich silks and precious gems. Very occasionally coins were specifically made for export, although examples are fairly scarce before the modern trade dollars of the nineteenth century. In the fourth century BC the Greek city of Cyzicus (quite near the Bosporus)

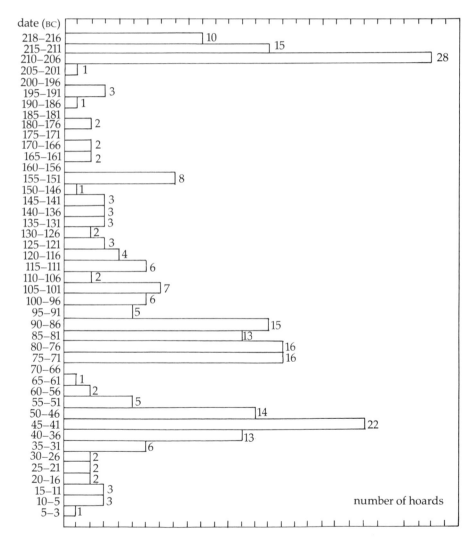

26 Hoards from Italy in the Roman Republic. This graph indicates peaks of non-recovery of hoards. Some of these coincide with warfare in Italy; others reflect periods of overseas wars, as a result of which soldiers who had been recruited in Italy were unable to return and recover their money.

made peculiarly archaic-looking coins of electrum, and these seem to have been intended for financing the corn trade between the Black Sea and Greece, as we can surmise from finds of them and from inscriptions. In a similar way, in the second century BC, some cities of Asia Minor made coins (e.g., fig. 6) of a weight standard which was heavier than that in force in the kingdom of Asia; it is no surprise that these coins all turn up in hoards outside Asia, mostly in northern Syria, where they were exported either as a political subsidy for the pretender Alexander Balas or as trade objects in exchange for goods, perhaps slaves.

The distribution of hoards might also be expected to reflect patterns of warfare and of wealth. For instance, it has often been thought that the progress of a military campaign, such as the invasions of the Germanic peoples into the northern Roman empire of the third and fourth centuries, could be plotted from the locations of hoards, or that areas with large numbers of hoards must have been relatively rich compared with other areas. But a study of the distribution of the hoards deposited in a well-documented period such as the English Civil War has shown that both of these assumptions are incorrect (fig. 27). The distribution of the hoards does not correspond with either population or wealth, in as much as these are revealed by documented figures such as the Ship Money Assessment of 1636. Nor can the hoards be closely related to the campaigns of the war. There are clusters around Newark and Gloucester, where there was fighting, but many hoards have been found in the north of England, where there was little, and there is no concentration in the important military region between London and Oxford. An attempt to reconstruct the history of the Civil War on the basis of the distribution of coin hoards would be very misleading, and we must guard against the temptation to do so for other, less well documented periods.

While the study of the chronological and geographical distribution of hoards can reveal fairly limited information of this kind, the analysis of their internal composition can reveal many important monetary and economic facts. The cardinal importance of hoards for establishing relative and absolute chronology has already been discussed in Chapter 2, but we can also use their composition for several other purposes, of which two will be described here.

First, we can use hoards to define the time individual coin types remained in circulation, since we can tell from them how long a particular coin continued to be available for hoarders. This sort of information is essential to the study of individual coin losses on a particular site or sites (see p. 49). We know, for instance, that the bulk of the bronze currency in circulation in the northern provinces of the Roman empire in the middle of the third century AD consisted of worn second-century sestertii only from the hoards that can be dated to those years. Typically these hoards have just one or two third-century coins, and a majority of second-century ones. In the same way we can also define short periods of currency life; it is from the composition of hoards that we know, for example, that neither of the two principal coinages of late twelfth- and thirteenth-century England, the Short Cross coinage of 1180–1247 and the Long Cross coinage of 1247–79, survived in circulation after their production had stopped.

A second use of the study of hoards is to provide information about the quantity of coins put into circulation (fig. 28). The principle underlying this approach is that if coins of year a are represented by x coins in hoards and

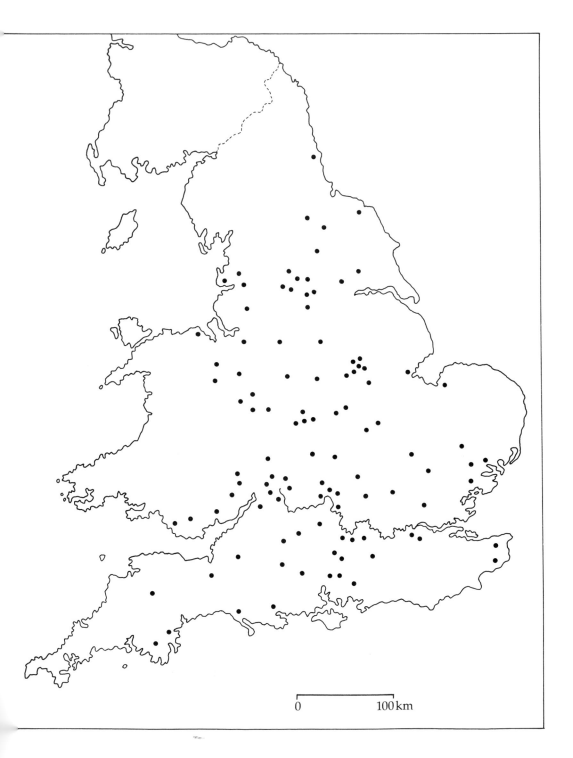

27 Hoards of the English Civil War. The distribution of hoards which were deposited in the Civil War does not closely reflect areas of fighting, nor does it correspond with regional variations in the density of population or wealth.

coins of year b are represented by $2x$ coins, then twice as many coins of year b were minted than of year a. On its own this principle provides information only about relative output, but it can be extended when used in conjunction with the estimation of the size of a coinage based on counting its dies (see p. 45). If the absolute size of certain selected issues can be established by counting their dies, it is possible to extrapolate similar values for other issues by comparing the representation of counted and uncounted issues in hoards. The most systematic use of this sort of approach has been in the study of the coinage of the last century of the Roman Republic.

However, many difficulties immediately suggest themselves with this use of hoards. One arises from the different ways hoards were put together (i.e. 'savings' or 'currency'); if the particular circumstances of a hoard's history affect the composition of two hoards with the same deposition dates, it is impossible for the composition of both to reflect mint output. Second, the method makes no allowance for the loss of coinage from circulation. If the x coins of year a were made, for example, a hundred years before the $2x$ coins of year b, it would be unwise to conclude that twice as many coins were made in year b, since to do so would take no account of the gradual wastage or erosion of coins of year a from circulation (by accidental loss, hoarding, export of coinage, melting down, etc.). In historical periods a loss factor of about 2 per cent per annum is known to have occurred; compounded over a period of as long as a century, this will clearly drastically reduce the amount of coinage of year a available to the hoarder at the later date.

Objections such as these are difficulties rather than fundamental flaws in the method, although, since the statistical methods devised to cope with them will depend on certain assumptions (for instance, a 2 per cent per annum erosion rate), the effect will be to reduce the degree of accuracy which can realistically be anticipated. But despite these problems the method receives powerful support from the practical comparison of the representation of coin issues in hoards and the size of those issues where they are known from mint records. The classic instance concerns a Swedish hoard of the eighteenth century from Lohe, the examination of which led to the establishment of the principle (fig. **28**), but much the same can be done for other well-documented periods such as seventeenth-century England. During the 1630s, for example, there is a high correlation between the amounts of each mint mark represented in hoards and the quantities of silver coinage available at each 'trial of the pyx', at which a fixed proportion of output was submitted for testing every year. Cases like this indicate the general validity of the method, although there is still a need to establish the limits of its accuracy.

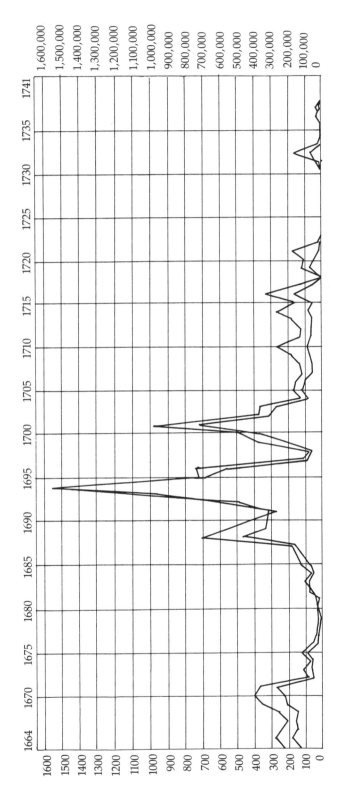

28 Hoards and mint output. This graph plots the representation by year (horizontal axis) in the eighteenth-century hoard from Lohe (Sweden) of coins of different years (left-hand axis) against the output of the mint for each year, as known from documentary sources (right-hand axis). It can be seen that there is a reasonable correlation.

— 5 —

Coins and the Past

The preceding chapters indicate the wealth of information which coins can contribute to our understanding of the past. Discussion of the methods of approaching the material has highlighted many of the problems which should be borne in mind when using coin evidence. These actually come down to common sense, but it still needs to be stressed that the successful study of coinage, as any other historical discipline, should be based on as full a collection of the evidence as possible as well as an awareness that this evidence should never be taken at face value. It is always necessary to set it against a more general background or to establish the conventions and limitations adopted by the makers of these small and almost two-dimensional objects.

There are also more general considerations. Coins do have considerable advantages over other objects as sources of information. They were officially produced, and thus often give information about official events which otherwise would not be known; the designs and legends they bear provide an unequalled number of images and inscriptions from lost societies. Second, and more important, they were mass-produced out of durable materials and so have survived in large numbers. This was one reason why they played such an important role in the renaissance of interest in the classical world from the fifteenth century onwards: here were many examples of objects giving tangible evidence for events which could otherwise only be read about. Moreover, the large number of coins which have survived and the way they have survived in hoards has made them the most datable objects from the ancient or medieval worlds that we possess. Although in terms of quantity more pottery has survived, it is the combination of the quantity of coins together with the official inscriptions and designs they bear that have made them more precisely datable than any other common class of artefact.

We use the study of coinage in default of and particularly to supplement other sources of historical information. Literary sources, Greek papyri, Roman inscriptions and medieval documents are generally more informative, even about monetary matters, than the coins themselves. The working of and motives for the closed currency system of the Hellenistic world are best understood from a papyrus of 258 BC. To take another example, we know that the ending in 1647 of the agreement between Spain and England, whereby Spain supplied much silver to be minted at London, is the explanation for the dramatic fall in output in that year. Yet this was a period when the English Civil War was at its height; from the coins themselves we would never have suspected that such a large proportion of minting in the war years of 1639–47 was the result of a commercial agreement between the two countries and not just of the high levels of expenditure caused by the war. The 1647 drop in production too might well have been mistakenly explained in terms of the course of the war.

The evidence of coins, as indeed of any artefact, is used as a source of history in inverse proportion to the amount of history which has survived. One would not use coins to try to make any deductions about economic history or matters such as liquidity if government statistics were available; one would not study the architecture of Roman temples from coins if the temples still survived. We might, of course, do the opposite, and try to explain the depictions of temples on coins or patterns of coin loss from our knowledge of surviving temples or official statistics for the money supply, but in this case we would be using coins as secondary evidence and not as a primary source of new information. Thus the importance of coinage for our understanding of the past diminishes, generally speaking, the more up to date we come. This tendency has been exacerbated by other factors too: the invention of new and more effective methods of communication, such as newspapers and television, has rendered the propaganda value of coinage less significant; technological changes, such as the invention of modern methods of factory production of coins, have tended to fossilise the significance of the designs they bear; and, particularly, the recent invention of new forms of money, including banknotes and credit cards, has enormously reduced the role played by coinage in the monetary and economic activity of modern states.

Further Reading

Several books give general surveys of coinage: see, for example, M. Price, (ed.) *Coins* (1980); P. Grierson, *Numismatics* (1975) or J. Cribb, I. Carradice and B. Cook, *The World Coin Atlas* (1990). Some books are devoted specifically to the sort of information which can be recovered from coins and the methodology of their study: M. Grant, *Roman History from Coins* (1958); John Casey, *Understanding Ancient Coins* (1986); M. H. Crawford, *Sources for Ancient History* (1983), chapter 4; and J. Casey and R. Reece (eds.), *Coins and the Archaeologist* (2nd edn 1988).

Up-to-date accounts of ancient and medieval coinages can be found in I. Carradice and M. Price, *Coinage in the Greek World* (1988); D. Nash, *Coinage in the Celtic World* (1987); A. Burnett, *Coinage in the Roman World* (1987); and P. Grierson and M. Blackburn, *Medieval European Coinage* (1986–). Much can be learnt from periods when there is a greater quantity of written information, and books such as C. E. Challis, *The Tudor Coinage* (1978), C. M. Cipolla, *Money in Sixteenth-Century Florence* (1986) and E. Besly, *English Civil War Coin Hoards* (1987) are very illuminating and can reveal many of the potential pitfalls of analysing coin evidence from earlier periods.

Other specialist studies, with more general applicability, are by M. Blackburn in C. J. Becker, (ed.), *Studies in the Coinages of the Eleventh Century* (1981), pp. 211ff (a die chain between imitative coins with different mint names); R. Reece, *Coinage in Roman Britain* (1987) (the study of site finds); T. R. Volk in G. Depeyrot, T. Hackens and G. Moucharte (eds.), *Rhythmes de la Production monétaire de l'Antiquité à nos Jours* (1987 [1990]), pp. 141–221 (the relationship between representation in hoards and mint output); D. R. Walker in B. W. Cunliffe (ed.), *The Temple of Sulis Minerva at Bath* 2 (1988), pp. 281–358 (estimation of the bronze coinage in circulation in Britain); W. Esty, *Numismatic Chronicle* 1986, pp. 185–215 (how to calculate die numbers from dies observed in a particular sample); M. Mate, *Numismatic Chronicle* 1969, pp. 207–18 and P. Kinns, *Numismatic Chronicle* 1983, pp. 1ff (both on average output per die); F. S. Kleiner, *The Arch of Nero in Rome* (1985) and M. Price and B. Trell, *Greek Coins and their Cities* (1977) (both on architectural types on coins); E. T. Hall and D. M. Metcalf (eds.), *Methods of Chemical and Metallurgical Investigations of Ancient Coinage* (1972).

Figure References

Illustrations are of coins held in the Department of Coins and Medals (CM, BMC) or Greek and Roman Antiquities (GR) in the British Museum, and copyright in the photographs belongs to the Trustees of the British Museum, unless otherwise noted.

1 CM 1984–5–39–1.
2 R. Hollingshead, *Chronicles of England, Scotland and Ireland* (1577).
3 CM E2315, 1915–5–7–2030.
4 CM 1988–7–42–5; 1948–6–2–6; 1860–3–30–332.
5 CM 1968–4–12–869; 1859–5–29–18.
6 BMC Smyrna 4; CM 1979–1–1–445.
8 M. H. Crawford, *Roman Republican Coin Hoards* (1969), table XIV (modified).
9 CM 1949–4–11–421; 1925–1–14–1; 1946–1–1–464.
10 BMC Metapontum 20; BMC Corinth 4.
11 Data from R. Bruce-Mitford, *The Sutton Hoo Ship-burial* I (1975), pp. 578–653.
12 CM 1970–9–9–83; 1970–9–9–84.
13 Boston Museum; Ars Classica XVI, 1598.
14 CM 1896–7–3–98.
15 BMC Republic 4030.
16 CM 1979–1–1–956.
17 BMC Augustus 599 and 508.
18 CM 1861–11–8–1; BMC Anastasius 1.
19 CM 1896–6–9–190; 1952–11–6–65.
20 CM 1870–5–7–37; 1919–9–18–1146.
21 BMC RC 30.
22 BMC Augustus 443; GR 1866.8–6.1.
23 Data from M. Mate, *Numismatic Chronicle* 1969, pp. 217–18.
24 Source: K. Hopkins, *Journal of Roman Studies* 1980, p. 109.
25 Source: R. Reece, *Coinage in Roman Britain* (1987), p. 83.
26 Source: M. Crawford, *Coinage and Money under the Roman Republic* (1985), p. 192.
27 Source: E. Besly, *English Civil War Coin Hoards* (1987), p. 61 (simplified).
28 Source: B. Thordeman, *Numismatic Chronicle* 1948, facing p. 204.

Index